Fishing
Glacier National Park

Help Us Keep This Guide Up to Date

Every effort has been made by the author and editors to make this guide as accurate and useful as possible. However, many things can change after a guide is published—trails are rerouted, regulations change, techniques evolve, facilities come under new management, etc.

We would love to hear from you concerning your experiences with this guide and how you feel it could be improved and kept up to date. Although we may not be able to respond to all comments and suggestions, we'll take them to heart and we'll also make certain to share them with the author. Please send your comments and suggestions to the following address:

The Globe Pequot Press
Reader Response/Editorial Department
P.O. Box 480
Guilford, CT 06437

Or you may e-mail us at:
editorial@GlobePequot.com

Thanks for your input, and happy travels!

Fishing
Glacier
National
Park

Second Edition

Russ Schneider

FALCONGUIDES ®

GUILFORD, CONNECTICUT
HELENA, MONTANA
AN IMPRINT OF ROWMAN & LITTLEFIELD

FALCONGUIDES®

All photos by Russ Schneider unless otherwise noted
Illustrations by Ashley A. Dean

Library of Congress Cataloging-in-Publication Data
Schneider, Russ
  Fishing Glacier National Park: your complete guide to more than 250 streams, rivers, and mountain lakes / by Russ Schneider.—2nd ed.
    p. cm.— (A Falcon guide)
  Includes bibliographical references (p.).
  ISBN 978-0-7627-1099-7
    1. Fishing—Montana—Glacier National Park—Guidebooks. 2. Glacier National Park (Mont.)—Guidebooks. I. title. II. Series.

SH517 .S34 2001
799.1'1'0978652—dc21

2001033123

Manufactured in the United States of America
Distributed by NATIONAL BOOK NETWORK

To buy books in quantity for corporate use
or incentives, call **(800) 962–0973**
or e-mail **premiums@GlobePequot.com.**

The author and Rowman & Littlefield assume no liability for accidents happening to, or injuries sustained by, readers who engage in the activities described in this book.

To Mom, of course

To *put a tenderfoot on spider bread, beans, bacon, and black coffee is often too severe; but when interspersed with plenty of trout and huckleberries picked in the valleys, that makes a perfect ration.*

—Albert L. Sperry, 1938

Contents

Map Legend xiv
Glacier National Park Overview Map xv
Foreword: Fishing at Sun Camp, by Monty Parratt xvi
Preface and Acknowledgments xviii
Introduction 1
How to Use This Guide 4
Essential Maps and Contacts 7
Vacation Planner 11
Fishing Glacier's Rivers 13
Fishing Glacier's Lakes 16
Daypack or Backpack Fishing Equipment 19
Resident Fish 21
North Fork of the Flathead River Drainage 32
    1. North Fork of the Flathead River 32
    2. Sage Creek 40
    3. Spruce Creek 40
    4. Kishenehn Creek 40
    5. Starvation Creek 41
    6. Kintla Creek 41
    7. Kintla Lake 41
    8. Upper Kintla Lake 42
    9. Agassiz Creek 42
  10. Red Medicine Bow Creek 43
  11. Ford Creek 43
  12. Parke Creek 43
  13. Long Bow Creek 43
  14. Long Bow Lake 43
  15. Numa Lake 44
  16. Numa Creek 44
  17. Akokala Creek 44
  18. Akokala Lake 44
  19. Pocket Lake 46
  20. Pocket Creek 46
  21. Jefferson Creek 46
  22. Bowman Lake 46
  23. Unnamed Lake (Lower Bowman) 47
  24. Bowman Creek 47
  25. Hidden Meadow Ponds 48
  26. Winona Lake 48
  27. Quartz Creek 48
  28. Lower Quartz Lake 48
  29. Middle Quartz Lake 49

30. Quartz Lake 49
31. Cerulean Lake 50
32. Gyrfalcon Lake 50
33. Cummings Creek 50
34. Logging Creek 52
35. Logging Lake 52
36. Grace Lake 53
37. Marian Lake 53
38. Unnamed Lake (Above Marian Lake) 54
39. Unnamed Lake (Below Trapper Peak) 54
40. Unnamed Lake (Adair Pond) 54
41. Unnamed Lake (Anaconda Pond) 54
42. Anaconda Creek 54
43. Anaconda Lake 54
44. Dutch Creek 54
45. Dutch Lakes 55
46. Ruger Lake 55
47. Camas Creek 55
48. McGee Creek 56
49. Rogers Lake 56
50. Trout Lake 56
51. Arrow Lake 57
52. Camas Lake 57
53. Lake Evangeline 58
54. Unnamed Ponds (Glacier Rim Area) 59
55. Unnamed Ponds (Lime Springs) 59

Waterton River Drainage 60
56. Waterton River 60
57. Waterton Lakes 60
58. Unnamed Lake (Thunderbird Pond) 63
59. Lake Francis 63
60. Lake Janet 64
61. Olson Creek 64
62. Cameron Lake 65
63. Boundary Creek 65
64. Lake Nooney 65
65. Lake Wurdeman 65
66. Carcajou Lake 65
67. Wahseeja Lake 65
68. Shaheeya Lake 65
69. Street Creek 65
70. Goat Haunt Lake 65
71. Cleveland Creek 66
72. Camp Creek 66

73. Kootenai Lakes 66
74. Stoney Indian Lake 67
75. Pass Creek 67
76. Kootenai Creek 68
77. Unnamed Lake (Lower Nahsukin) 68
78. Nahsukin Lake 68
79. Unnamed Lake (Upper Nahsukin) 68
80. Bench Lake 68
81. Redhorn Lake 68
82. South Fork of Valentine Creek 68
83. Valentine Creek 69

Belly River Drainage 70
84. Belly River 70
85. Miche Wabun Lake 74
86. North Fork of the Belly River 74
87. Kaina Lake 74
88. Whitecrow Creek 74
89. Whitecrow Lake 74
90. Atsina Lake 74
91. Sue Lake 74
92. Ipasha Lake 74
93. Unnamed Lake (Above Ipasha Lake) 74
94. Margaret Lake 75
95. Mokowanis River 75
96. Mokowanis Lake 76
97. Glenns Lake 76
98. Cosley Lake 77
99. Helen Lake 78
100. Unnamed Lake (Below Old Sun Glacier) 78
101. Elizabeth Lake 78

McDonald Creek Drainage 80
102. McDonald Creek 80
103. Lake McDonald 82
104. Apgar Creek 83
105. Fern Creek 83
106. Fish Creek 83
107. Howe Creek 84
108. Upper Howe Lake 84
109. Lower Howe Lake 85
110. Sprague Creek 85
111. Jackson Creek 85
112. Fish Lake 87
113. Johns Lake 87
114. Feather Woman Lake 87

115. Akaiyan Lake 87
116. Snyder Creek 87
117. Lower Snyder Lake 88
118. Upper Snyder Lake 88
119. Avalanche Creek 88
120. Avalanche Lake 88
121. Unnamed Lake (Below Sperry Glacier) 89
122. Unnamed Lake (Sperry Campground Pond) 89
123. Hidden Creek 89
124. Hidden Lake 90
125. Logan Creek 90
126. Mineral Creek 90
127. Longfellow Creek 91
128. Continental Creek 91
Saint Mary River Drainage 92
129. Saint Mary River 92
130. Saint Mary Lake 93
131. Reynolds Creek 98
132. Siyeh Creek 98
133. Twin Lakes 98
134. Gunsight Lake 98
135. Virginia Creek 98
136. Baring Creek 100
137. Lost Lake 100
138. Goat Lake 100
139. Otokomi Lake 100
140. Rose Creek 101
141. Red Eagle Creek 101
142. Red Eagle Lake 102
143. Hudson Creek 103
144. Medicine Owl Creek 103
145. Medicine Owl Lake 103
146. Unnamed Lake (Upper Divide Creek Lakes) 103
147. Divide Creek 103
148. Boulder Lakes 104
149. Boulder Creek 104
150. Unnamed Lake (Below Flattop Ridge) 104
151. Unnamed Lake (Below Wynn Mountain) 104
152. Unnamed Lake (Boulder Ridge #1) 104
153. Unnamed Lake (Boulder Ridge #2) 104
154. Cracker Lake 105
155. Allen Creek 105
156. Canyon Creek 105
157. Falling Leaf Lake 105

158. Snow Moon Lake 105
159. Unnamed Lake (Allen Mountain Ponds) 105
160. Cataract Creek 105
161. Upper Grinnell Lake 106
162. Grinnell Lake 106
163. Lake Josephine 106
164. Stump Lake 106
165. Swiftcurrent Creek 107
166. Windmaker Lake 107
167. Upper Bullhead Lake 107
168. Lower Bullhead Lake 107
169. Red Rock Lake 108
170. Fishercap Lake 108
171. Iceberg Lake 108
172. Unnamed Lake (Below Mount Wilbur) 109
173. Wilbur Creek 109
174. Ptarmigan Lake 109
175. Swiftcurrent Lake 109
176. Natahki Lake 110
177. Apikuni Creek 110
178. Lake Sherburne 110
179. Governor Pond 111
180. Unnamed Lake (Sherburne South Shore Pond) 111
181. Swiftcurrent Ridge Lake 111
182. Kennedy Lake 111
183. Kennedy Creek 111
184. Poia Lake 111
185. Unnamed Lake (Yellow Mountain Pond) 112
186. Otatso Lakes 112
187. Otatso Creek 112
188. Slide Lake 112
189. Lower Slide Lake 112
190. Lee Creek 112
191. Jule Creek 113

North Fork of Cut Bank Creek Drainage 114
192. North Fork of Cut Bank Creek 114
193. Unnamed Lake (Amphitheater Basin) 114
194. Pitamakan Lake 114
195. Lake of the Winds 114
196. Katoya Lake 114
197. Morning Star Lake 116
198. Medicine Grizzly Lake 116
199. Unnamed Lakes (Below Medicine Grizzly Peak) 118
200. Atlantic Creek 118

201. Lonely Lakes 118
202. Running Crane Lake 118
203. Lake Creek 118
Two Medicine River Drainage 119
204. Two Medicine River 119
205. Lower Two Medicine Lake 119
206. Two Medicine Lake 119
207. Pray Lake 121
208. Upper Two Medicine Lake 121
209. Unnamed Lake (Upper Two Medicine Pond) 122
210. Oldman Lake 122
211. Young Man Lake 124
212. Boy Lake 124
213. Unnamed Lake (Below Red Mountain) 124
214. Sky Lake 124
215. Unnamed Lake (Below Rising Wolf #1) 124
216. Unnamed Lake (Below Rising Wolf #2) 124
217. Dry Fork 124
218. No Name Lake 124
219. Colbalt Lake 125
220. Aster Creek 125
221. Paradise Creek 125
222. Appistoki Creek 125
223. Fortymile Creek 125
224. Fortyone Mile Creek 125
225. Midvale Creek 125
226. Railroad Creek 126
227. Unnamed Lake (South Fork of Railroad Creek) 126
228. Lubec Lake 126
229. Lena Lake 126
230. Coonsa Creek 126
231. Green Lake 126
232. Summit Lake 126
233. Three Bears Lake 126
234. Summit Creek 127
Middle Fork of the Flathead River Drainage 128
235. Middle Fork of the Flathead River 128
236. Autumn Creek 136
237. Bear Creek 136
238. Jackstraw Lake 136
239. Unnamed Lake (Upper Ole Creek) 136
240. Ole Creek 136
241. Fielding Creek 137
242. Debris Creek 137

243. Ole Lake 137
244. Unnamed Lake (Below Brave Dog Mountain) 138
245. Upper Lake Isabel 138
246. Lake Isabel 138
247. Aurice Lakes 139
248. Striped Elk Lake 139
249. Park Creek 139
250. Unnamed Lake (Salvage Basin) 139
251. Muir Creek 139
252. Coal Creek 139
253. Elk Creek 140
254. Unnamed Lake (Below Cloudcroft Peak) 140
255. Pinchot Creek 140
256. Buffalo Woman Lake 140
257. Beaver Woman Lake 140
258. Nyack Lakes 140
259. Stimson Lake 140
260. Unnamed Lake (Stimson Creek) 141
261. Unnamed Lakes (Thompson Lakes #1 & #2) 141
262. Thompson Creek 141
263. Nyack Creek 141
264. Halfmoon Lake 141
265. Harrison Creek 141
266. Harrison Lake 141
267. Lincoln Creek 143
268. Walton Creek 143
269. Lincoln Lake 143
270. Lake Ellen Wilson 144
271. Rubideau Creek 144

Resources 145
Select Bibliography 147
Index 149
About the Author 155

Map Legend

US Highway	89	Fishing Site	2
State or Other Principal Road	17	Bridge	
Paved Road		Campground	▲
Gravel Road		Cabin or Building	▪
Unimproved Road		Ranger Station	
Trail/Route		Peak	**X** 5,281 ft.
Trailhead	T	Pass	)(
Lake, River/Creek, Waterfalls		National or State Forest/Park Boundary	
Boat Landing			
Marsh or Wetland		Map Orientation	N
Glacier		Scale	0 0.5 1 Miles

Glacier National Park Overview Map

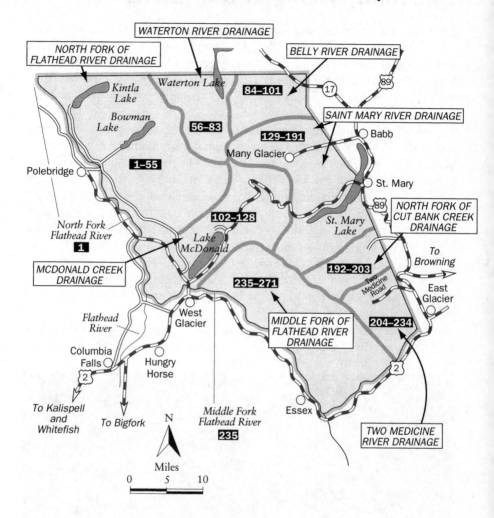

WATERTON RIVER DRAINAGE

NORTH FORK OF FLATHEAD RIVER DRAINAGE

BELLY RIVER DRAINAGE

Kintla Lake

Waterton Lake

84–101

17

89

Bowman Lake

56–83

SAINT MARY RIVER DRAINAGE

129–191

Babb

Many Glacier

St. Mary

1–55

Polebridge

North Fork Flathead River

1

102–128

St. Mary Lake

89

NORTH FORK OF CUT BANK CREEK DRAINAGE

Lake McDonald

MCDONALD CREEK DRAINAGE

To Browning

192–203

East Glacier

Two Medicine Road

235–271

West Glacier

204–234

Flathead River

MIDDLE FORK OF FLATHEAD RIVER DRAINAGE

2

Columbia Falls

Hungry Horse

2

To Kalispell and Whitefish

To Bigfork

N

Middle Fork Flathead River

235

Essex

TWO MEDICINE RIVER DRAINAGE

Miles

0   5   10

Foreword: Fishing at Sun Camp

My father, Lloyd Parratt, was summertime ranger naturalist in the Saint Mary Valley from the years 1944 to 1963. Our family had the unique opportunity to live in government housing at Sun Camp Ranger Station. Sun Camp Ranger Station was a log cabin built in the 1930s down by Baring Falls. Baring Creek ran right beside my window, set in the ever-changing solitude of Saint Mary Lake.

My brother Mark and I were ardent fishermen and took on many challenges that the wilderness of Glacier National Park handed us. Most of our years fishing were on the east side of the Continental Divide near Saint Mary Lake. We fished with bait most times. We sometimes had as much fun catching grasshoppers and finding maggots in old carcasses as we did fishing. We caught mostly whitefish and lake trout in front of the Sun Camp Ranger Station. We would almost always catch our limit of whitefish, but once in a while the whitefish would suddenly stop biting. Then, we would go get our father. He would put his rubber hip waders on and walk out into the rift of Baring Creek. Three or four casts with a Daredevle and Dad would have one of those mammoth lake trout on the line while his rod made that distinctive pulsating action.

As Mark and I grew older we would troll for the "big ones" down deep with the oversized Daredevle. Occasionally, we would hook up with one of

In this 1953 photo, young Monty Parratt, left, and his brother Mark hold an early Saint Mary Lake trout. LLOYD PARRATT PHOTO

those awesome creatures and end up with a fish tale that most would not believe. Some big Mackinaws (lake trout) tugged us around for what felt like an hour. The largest one we ever caught was over forty pounds, which Mark reeled in. We did catch several fish in the fifteen- to twenty-five-pound range.

Sometimes when the wind was blowing a mist off Saint Mary Lake, we would hike to Saint Mary Falls above the lake to fish. We would fish over ledges with thirty feet of line out. The water was fast and the fish were feeding at the bottom twenty feet below the surface. The trick was to get your bait down and keep it down. We dragged in many whitefish this way.

We ate every fish we caught and sometimes kept the fish alive in an old washtub in the shower with a window screen over it and the cold water from the shower flowing continuously from Baring Falls. The meltwater from Sexton Glacier, on the cirque between Going-to-the-Sun and Matipi Mountains, fed the rich waters of Baring Creek and our bathtub.

In our early years, Mark and I explored every square mile, every stream, and every fishing hole of the Saint Mary Valley, the Belly River, the North Fork, and as much of Glacier National Park as we could. What an incredible place to grow up and to fish. I hope that you can explore some of those holes, too.

Monty Parratt
Retired teacher, Veteran of the Blister Rust Campaign
and many summers fishing in Glacier National Park

Preface and Acknowledgments

Kim and I were sitting at Otokomi Lake this past summer, she poring over the map, while I put together our fly rods, when she said, "Russ, did you know that Goat Lake is twice as big as Otokomi?" It made me think of all the waters I had left out of the first edition of this book, for various reasons: They were closed, fishless, I didn't want to highlight them, didn't know much about the fishing there, etc. With this in mind, in this edition of Fishing Glacier National Park I have included all major streams, rivers, and lakes, as well as most of the minor ones regardless of their fishing opportunities. I am sure you will find a few potholes and smaller streams I missed, but I tried to produce as complete a document on the park's fisheries as I could without spending the rest of my life on one edition.

Originally, I undertook this project because I felt that having visited and fished most of the major fishing areas in the park, both as a guide and as a lover of Glacier, I could share this land and the special fishing experience it provides. I hope that as you read and then fish in the park you appreciate how important it is to preserve fishing opportunities in Glacier National Park. When your kids and your grandkids visit the park with you, they should still be able to catch wild cutthroat and hopefully someday bull trout again. You can help the preservation of Glacier's native fisheries by learning to carefully identify native fish and releasing them in sensitive waters, but more important, by not releasing any invasive, non-native species you catch.

Without support from Kim, this revision would have never made it to press.

The descriptions in this book are based on my experience as a backpacking guide in Glacier National Park and as a fishing guide on the North and Middle Forks of the Flathead River, an extensive survey of existing fisheries research and literature on the park, and the suggestions of knowledgeable anglers and biologists. I have done my best to compile as much information as possible about the waters of Glacier. However, although the result is based on the most reliable and educated sources, in the end, all of the information contained in this guide is solely my best estimate of the fishing conditions, species present, and so forth. It does not necessarily represent the opinion of the National Park Service, U.S. Fish and Wildlife Service, Montana Department of Fish, Wildlife, and Parks, or anyone else. For those of you who want to take your GPS and find a little-visited lake, just to see if it has fish, I salute you and hope to aid in your quest.

I hope someday to appreciate the park as much as those who lived it all their lives and shared it with me. Monty Parratt especially deserves my thanks for writing the Foreword, only a sliver of his many Glacier adventures. Mark Parratt gets the prize for, to my knowledge, the biggest fish caught in Glacier. Many people made this book better, and many people made me better, as an angler and a guide. Thanks especially to Bill Michels, Carolyn Beecher, Cris Coughlin, Denny Gignoux, Don McCann, Doug Betters, Eric Hanson, Ev Lundgren, Irv Heitz, Jim Vashro, John Gray, Leo Marnell, Michael S. Sample, Randy Gayner, Rusty Wells, Steve Smith, and Wade Fredenberg.

I am forever indebted to Mike Block and Doug Niemann for teaching me to row. I love to row.

Most important, thank you, family.

And to Kim, I wish you many happy bushwhacking trips in Glacier. May I never be too old and slow to keep up.

Introduction

May 11, 1910: Glacier National Park became an officially designated preserve and playground for outdoor enthusiasts. With over one million acres within its boundaries and two million acres of the Bob Marshall Wilderness to the south, it is part of the largest wilderness in the lower 48 states. The National Park Service estimates that there are 131 officially named lakes and some 631 unnamed lakes in Glacier National Park. Countless creeks flow from and through these lakes into eight major drainages that flow into three different oceans and harbor twenty-six different species of fish. Glacier may be better known for its scenery and the Going-to-the-Sun Road than for its fishing, but its waters offer everything from whitefish, brook trout, and cutthroat trout to the possibility of state record cutthroat-rainbow trout hybrid, lake trout, brook trout, or arctic grayling.

Whether you keep your fish or not, Glacier has a fishing trip for everyone. You can try to get a large cutthroat-rainbow hybrid out of Red Eagle Lake, or you can get fish after fish to take your ugliest fly or lure at Ole, Snyder, or Lake Isabel. If you want challenging stream fishing, try Cut Bank Creek or the Belly River. If you want a guide, hire one and try fly-fishing the North and Middle Forks of the Flathead, or try a worm and a smile on Lower Two Medicine Lake. The fish will keep you happy.

The park has always been a great place to hike and catch trout in a wild setting. Having fished many waters in Montana, I appreciate the lack of crowds at most backcountry lakes in Glacier, an experience that is due to the regulating of backcountry visits by the National Park Service. A backcountry permit is required for all overnight trips, and you must stay at designated campgrounds. Campsites are grouped in small clusters, so your backcountry experience will likely involve other campers, but backcountry use is kept at a constant level, which makes backcountry fisheries management easier for the National Park Service. Day-use areas, on the other hand, receive increased pressure with increased visitation. For example, Hidden Lake is only 3 miles from the Logan Pass Visitor Center, the main destination of 90 percent of park visitors. It receives intense pressure from day-trip anglers. Unfortunately, the trail has been closed numerous times in recent years due to conflicts between anglers who want to keep the fish they catch and grizzlies attracted to the smell. Current regulations prohibit keeping the fish you catch at Hidden Lake. This progression is a warning to anglers in other areas of the park who do not take precautions to prevent bear problems.

Anglers who leave a mess endanger the next visitor and endanger fishing in Glacier. I recommend catch-and-release for most areas, but you can still catch and eat a fish in the park. Ideally, catch fish about a mile or two from camp, clean and fillet the fish where you caught them (hopefully a reasonable distance from camp), and throw the entrails into deep water away from camp.

Lake trout, like this one taken from Lake McDonald, have proven detrimental to native fish west of the Continental Divide.

Keep transport time to a minimum, but also keep the smelly process of cleaning fish away from camp. There is no perfect way to reduce impact in the backcountry, but if everybody makes an effort to be as clean a visitor as possible, we all benefit.

The native fish of Glacier may not be as essential a link to other wildlife as, say, Alaska's salmon, but they do furnish loons, eagles, and sometimes people with valuable food. Although it is hard to imagine, many high mountain lakes have no fish. You can sit beside Dutch Lake all day and not see a single cutthroat rising or cruising, although before 1972 an official program stocked many lakes in the park, such as Dutch, Camas, Ptarmigan, and Poia. Some of the stocked populations survived, as did the Yellowstone cutthroat populations of Evangeline and Camas Lakes and the rainbow population in Ptarmigan. Many did not reproduce, however, and the lakes reverted to their unpopulated condition.

Some anglers think that stocking a fishless lake is a good thing, and they are right. It is a good thing for them in the short term, but later, when lake trout and rainbow trout out-compete the native cutthroat and bull trout, the native fish get closer to extinction and fishing for them ends. Anglers are the easiest to blame for bucket biologist problems, but Yellowstone cutthroat were stocked in many Glacier National Park waters as late as 1954, and official stocking programs of westslope cutthroat trout continued until around 1972. Consequently, only in more isolated lakes do genetically pure westslope cutthroat populations prosper.

The National Park Service no longer stocks the waters of Glacier. Today the emphasis is on ensuring the future survival of the park's unique native fishes for the benefit and enjoyment of future generations. If you want a fat, stocked rainbow, try Duck Lake on the Blackfeet Indian Reservation, but if you want to catch and release a native cutthroat in its natural habitat in one of the prettiest places on the planet, try the lakes and rivers of Glacier National Park.

How to Use This Guide

This guide will help you plan your next fishing excursion in Glacier. I have organized the information under the following headings:

Location: To avoid confusion about which water is specified by each site, a sample waypoint is included. These waypoints are intended to be map precise; that is, they should take you to the exact spot on the map you want and should prevent any confusion between lakes. However, these waypoints are not intended to be your only source for finding off-trail lakes and streams. If you intend to visit a remote stream or lake, obtain the U.S. Geological Survey (USGS) 7.5-minute quadrangle for the area you plan to visit. Calculate multiple waypoints for your entire route and enter them into your GPS unit. Then, when you get to the trailhead, track your progress with additional waypoints and compare those to your map-precise entries. This book uses Universal Transverse Mercator (UTM) coordinates (the coordinates of the mouth of the stream where it flows into the larger stream or river or the foot or outlet of the lake). UTM coordinates tend to be more GPS friendly and user-friendly coordinate systems than latitude and longitude or township and range. The new Glacier National Park USGS map includes 1,000-meter tick marks. UTM uses these standard reference points to grid maps into 1,000-meter intervals (1,000 meters equals approximately 0.62 mile).

Elevation: At the level of the lake, obtained from USGS maps of the park.

Area or Length: Acres for known lakes are provided by Montana USGS and the National Park Service; miles for streams and rivers are compiled from Montana Natural Resource Information Systems (nris.state.mt.us). N/A means information was not available at the time of publication.

Species: Species listings are the best estimates of the author based on a combination of firsthand knowledge; my evaluation of research by the Montana Department of Fish, Wildlife, and Parks; Montana Natural Resource Information Systems (nris.state.mt.us); the U.S. Fish and Wildlife Service; and the National Park Service. Species are listed in order of their abundance at each site. These approximations do not represent the official opinions of any of these agencies but rather the author's combined assessment of the results of the respective research.

Species are represented by the following abbreviations:

AG	arctic grayling
BT	bull trout
EBT	brook trout
KS	Kokanee or land-locked salmon
LC	Ling cod (burbot)
LT	lake trout
LWF	lake whitefish

Some boat ramps, such as this one at Glacier Rim River Access, require four-wheel drive.

MWF	mountain whitefish
NP	northern pike
CRT	cutthroat-rainbow hybrid
RS	redside shiner
RT	rainbow trout
WCT	westslope cutthroat trout
YCT	Yellowstone cutthroat trout

Relative population density estimates by the author are indicated as follows:

A	abundant
C	common
R	rare

In addition to the native and non-native fishes listed above, various sculpins and other minnows, some native, some not, inhabit the park's waters. See the table on native fish later in this section.

Two icons are used to denote that lakes and streams have no fish or that the status of the fish population is unknown.

Fishless

Status unknown

Site Descriptions: Each water, with the exception of small streams, fishless waters, small tarns, and seasonal ponds, has descriptions containing information such as the best time to fish; a brief overview of the fishing site and the fishing experience, based on my personal perspective and the experiences of others who have visited the same spot; useful equipment such as float tubes and rafts; site-specific information on flies, lures, and the best spots to fish; and access information where relevant.

The locator maps that accompany each section will also help, but please refer to the USGS map of Glacier National Park and UTM coordinates for exact locations and how to reach them. For the backcountry campsites and complete trail descriptions, see *Hiking Glacier and Waterton Lakes National Parks,* by Erik Molvar (Falcon, 1994).

Essential Maps and Contacts

In addition to this book, you will need two maps, fishing regulations, and perhaps a backcountry permit and camping guide to plan your fishing vacation in Glacier National Park.

USGS 1:100,000-scale topographic map of Glacier National Park (recently updated; if you plan to bushwhack off-trail you'll need the 7.5-minute quads).

USGS
U.S. Department of the Interior/U.S. Geological Survey
12201 Sunrise Valley Drive
Reston, VA 20192
mapping.usgs.gov

Three Forks of the Flathead River Map
Glacier National Park Conservancy
P.O. Box 310
West Glacier, MT 59936
(406) 888–5756
gnha@glacierassociation.org

Backcountry camping guide, camping permits, and current regulations. Most of this information is available on the park's award-winning Web site.

Glacier National Park
P.O. Box 128
West Glacier, MT 59936
(406) 888–7800 (voice)
(406) 888–7896 (TDD)
www.nps.gov/glac
glac_info@nps.gov

GLACIER'S FISHING REGULATIONS

These regulations were applicable at the time of this printing; check current regulations.

1. Obtain a copy of the current regulations at entrance stations and visitor centers.
2. No license is required for fishing in Glacier.
3. A Montana fishing license is required for float fishing the North Fork of the Flathead River. Wade-fishing on the west side of the North Fork and fishing anywhere on the Middle Fork also require a Montana fishing license. Wade-fishing on the park side of either river does not require a

license. The Montana Department of Fish, Wildlife, and Parks has made the entire Flathead River drainage (not including park tributaries and lakes) catch-and-release for cutthroat.

4. A Blackfeet Tribal Permit is required for fishing on all tribal waters, including fishing from a boat in either Lake Sherburne or Lower Two Medicine Lake and fishing Cut Bank Creek or the Lower Saint Mary River just outside the park. Tribal permits are available at some fishing outfitters in the Flathead Valley and several convenience stores on the reservation. Check current regulations and be advised that using a float tube and/or a boat requires purchasing additional permits.

5. Fishing for bull trout is illegal, and any bull trout caught incidentally must be immediately released.

6. Always check current regulations.

BLACKFEET TRIBAL PERMITS

Permits are required for all non-tribal members engaging in any recreational activity, including fishing outside the park on the east side. Historically, the tribe requires the purchase of a conservation permit, a fishing permit, and a float tube or boat permit if applicable.

Blackfeet Fish and Game Department
P.O. Box 850
Browning, MT 59417
(406) 338–7207

LEAD WEIGHTS

I do not recommend the use of lead weights, and neither does the National Park Service. It may be illegal in the near future to use lead weights, and increasingly sporting goods manufacturers are making weights made of innocuous alloys instead. Every year loons and other waterfowl die of lead poisoning from eating lead fish sinkers and jigs. Lead sinkers and jigs can be lost in water if caught on rocks, logs, or weeds. Waterfowl often get their food by digging in the mud at the bottom of lakes and may accidentally eat lost lead fishing gear. Lead breaks down in a bird's gizzard and disperses into the bloodstream, causing damage to its organs and brain. The bird often becomes sick and dies or is unable to produce offspring.

GLACIER'S HIKING REGULATIONS

These regulations were applicable at the time of this printing; check current regulations.

1. No permit is required for day hiking.

2. All backpackers must obtain a backcountry camping permit, available at visitor centers; check current regulations.

3. Backcountry camping is allowed only in designated campgrounds, which allow a maximum of four campers per tent site. Each campground has between two and ten tent sites.
4. Undesignated camping requires special permission of the district ranger and is subject to severe limitations. An exception to this rule is the Nyack—Coal Creek undesignated camping area. However, as of this printing there were few waters in that area open to fishing. Camping permits may be obtained from the backcountry permit station at the Saint Mary Visitor Center, at the Backcountry Permit Center in Apgar, or from park headquarters.

FISHING AND BEARS

Anglers can make their trips in bear country safer by taking a few extra precautions:
1. Remember that bears like to travel along streams and lakeshores, so when following either—especially a loudly rushing mountain stream— in thick brush, clap your hands, sing, or make some other noise, preferably metallic.
2. Catch-and-release fishing is much less likely to attract a bear than cooking fish for dinner. If you want fish for dinner, leave your catch in the water as long as possible to keep the smell to a minimum.
3. Do not clean fish in camp. Clean fish at the nearest body of water, preferably where you caught them. Avoid transporting fish for long distances in bear country. Fillet them at the shore and, after puncturing the air bladder, toss the entrails, heads, and bones into deep water. This leaves no leftovers. After eating, toss excess bones and skin into the deepest part of the water. Dispose of entrails 200 feet from any trail or campground in deep water. Pack out all tin foil and other garbage. Do not burn or bury.
4. Never leave entrails along lakeshores or in streams.
5. Avoid getting fish odors on your clothes, and wash your hands thoroughly after cleaning fish. If you do get fish guts or smell on your clothes, don't take them into your tent; hang them with your food.
6. For a more thorough discussion of safe camping in bear country, see *Bear Aware,* by Bill Schneider (Falcon, 2001).

FISHING AND FLOATING COURTESY: BE A GOOD SPORT

Riverboat Users

1. Be organized before you approach the launch area.
2. Allow space between your boat and others when fishing.
3. Watch for wading anglers and plan a path to avoid them, their fishing lines, and their fishing holes.

4. Do not drag an anchor or chain on streambeds.

Anglers

1. Do not crowd other anglers. Keep out of sight of others, if possible.
2. Let others enjoy good fishing spots, too.
3. Yield to boats when there is no other channel for the boater to navigate.
4. Avoid using the streambed as a pathway.

Source: River Recreation Conflicts Group, Ethics and Education Committee, *Montana Fishing Regulations* (Helena, Mont.: Montana Department of Fish, Wildlife, and Parks, 1998).

Vacation Planner

Lots of action, but not necessarily big fish or easy hikes
Lost Lake
Ole Lake
Lake Isabel
Snyder Lakes
Most low-elevation creeks

Challenging fishing for large fish
Red Eagle Lake
Oldman Lake
Arrow Lake
Glenns Lake

Motor boat trolling
Saint Mary Lake
Lake McDonald
Waterton Lake
Bowman Lake
Two Medicine Lake

Realistic hike and fish day trips
Red Rock Lake
Josephine Lake
Upper Two Medicine Lake
Snyder Lakes
Lower Quartz Lake
Kootenai Lakes
Belly River
Howe Lakes
Avalanche Lake
Saint Mary River
Trout Lake
Cut Bank Creek

Long hike and fish day trips
Quartz Lake
Oldman Lake
Otokomi Lake
Red Eagle Lake
Gunsight Lake
Akokala Lake
Medicine Grizzly Lake

Backcountry lake trout
Cosley Lake
Glenns Lake

Drive to canoe and fish lakes
Two Medicine Lake
Bowman Lake
Kintla Lake
Winona Lake
Lake Sherburne

Float fishing on a river
Middle Fork of the Flathead River
North Fork of the Flathead River

Wade-fishing in a river
Middle Fork of the Flathead River
North Fork of the Flathead River
Waterton River
Belly River
Two Medicine River
McDonald Creek

Extended backpacking and fishing vacations
Gunsight, Ellen Wilson, and Snyder Lakes
Lincoln and Harrison Lakes
Grace and Logging Lakes
Camas Lake
Quartz and Lower Quartz Lakes
Kintla, Francis, and Kootenai Lakes
Belly River, Mokowanis, and Kootenai Lakes
Cut Bank Creek, Medicine Grizzly Lake, Red Eagle Lake

Fishing Glacier's Rivers

River fishing in Glacier is not as good as on some of Montana's famous rivers, but all three forks of the Flathead still produce a few large fish and can provide lots of action. The Belly, Waterton, and Saint Mary Rivers also offer river fishing, although not from a boat. Their respective descriptions give more information about these waters, but following are a few words on river fishing techniques.

The fish populations of rivers depend on the amount of nutrients in the water, the availability of spawning beds, and the level of predation. Rivers in Glacier have clear, clean water with some glacial flour, a fine film of ground-up sediment scoured from rock by glacial ice. Unlike some famous tailwater fisheries such as the Missouri and Bighorn Rivers, the waters of Glacier's rivers are almost too clean to support large populations of big fish. The nutrient-poor waters mean that fish cannot be very picky when choosing a meal. Fish in Glacier will focus on a major hatch, if available, but are generally more receptive to attractor patterns than are fish in nutrient-rich waters.

As far as lures are concerned, I've done my share of lure fishing and have historically had good luck with red-and-white Daredevles and gold Thomas Cyclones with red-and-white spots. If you want to expand your arsenal, though, include some Panther Martins, rooster tails, Mepps, Krocodiles, and smaller flashy lures.

The best way to work the North and Middle Forks is from a boat.

DISARM THAT TREBLE HOOK

If you fish with lures, cut two of the treble hooks off and bend the barb of the remaining hook down to allow for easy, painless release of the cutthroat and bull trout. Worms almost always work but often kill the fish. If you are fishing with worms, fish only until you take your limit and try not to fish where there are bull trout. There is one thing worth noting about lure-fishing in an area that is heavily fly-fished: Fly-fishing is definitely the norm on the rivers, and most fly-fishers seem to develop a disdain of the spin angler. However, there is little evidence that a spin angler who cuts two treble hooks off his or her lure kills any more fish than the fly fisherman does. And, specific to this ecosystem, a lure angler is more likely to catch and keep a lake trout, a fish ambivalent to most flies.

PRESENTATION FOR GLACIER'S RIVERS

Generally there is more room for error when fishing in a river, because the current skews a fish's view of the fly or lure. This allows the use of bigger,

FLY AND LURE SUGGESTIONS FOR GLACIER'S RIVERS

Generally I still feel good about recommending the same flies I did in the first edition, with a couple exceptions and additions. Instead of a size 12 parachute Adams, you may need a 14 or a 16 as the water clears and fish see a lot of orange stimulators. In addition, fish have become a lot pickier about which stimulator they will take, and you will be wise to try variations from the norm.

Flies: orange stimulator, parachute Adams, yellow humpy, olive elk hair caddis, olive woolly bugger, various hopper patterns, bead-head pheasant tail, bead-head hare's ear, Zug bug, olive sculpin pattern, small bead-head girdle bug with clipped short rubber legs, and, for muddy water, purple egg-sucking leech

Lures: red-and-white or gold Mepps, yellow Warden rooster tails, gold and rainbow Thomas Cyclones, red-and-white Daredevles, black-and-green or rainbow Krocodiles, black-and-yellow Panther Martins, large orange-and-silver spoons for lake trout, green jigs

Bait: worms, hoppers, crickets, corn, marshmallows, and pieces of cheese rather than coated, overpriced bait. Regarding bait, check current regulations, because as fishing pressure increases bait-fishing is often prohibited. Generally, it is not a good idea to fish with bait in waters inhabited by bull trout; however, bait-fishing is also an effective way to remove lake trout from an aquatic environment in which they may be competing with bull trout. Use your best judgment and a single hook. *Regulations prohibit collecting bait in the park.*

heavily hackled flies that float longer. When fly-fishing, try to match size and color of the most common food insects and forage fish.

When spin-fishing, do not reel a lure on an unnatural course or at an unnatural speed. Reel at a moderate speed and stop periodically for a couple of seconds to imitate the behavior of a resting fish. If you feel a bite or see a fish chasing your lure, a spurt of speed can be the last bit of incentive the fish needs to go for your lure. If you are floating, keep your rod tip high so as not to lose or snag lures on the bottom. In early season, fish in the eddies behind rocks and other slow water. Spring runoff is fast and full of sediment, so fish will not hold in the main current or in the long runs.

Also cast to the shallow waters if fishing dry flies. Cutthroats avoid predators like bull or lake trout by staying in the shallows during periods of murky water. If you are fishing wet flies or lures, use something big and ugly and brighter than normal.

As the season progresses, the water drops and clears and fishing with dry flies becomes increasingly effective. Less gaudy lures are more productive. Rainbows, especially, move into the long runs with large boulders for cover and medium current. Cutthroats stay in the pools and shallower corners but range more into the flats and slightly faster water. Whitefish and lake trout stay along the bottom, feeding on aquatic insects and poor little cutthroat, respectively.

Fishing Glacier's Lakes

Glacier National Park was named not for its glaciers but for its glacially carved valleys with strings of lakes, either round and deep or long and slender. The National Park Service estimates that there are 131 officially named lakes and some 631 unnamed lakes in Glacier National Park (721 lakes registered on a GIS query of lakes in the park, but the majority were less than an acre in size). These lakes support fish from the smallest cutthroats to the biggest rainbows and lake trout. Few of the lakes in Glacier are closed to fishing, and many are within a day's hike by trail.

I fished my first mountain lake when I was six, with the attitude that the only reason to hike was to get to good fishing. I modified that philosophy somewhat a couple of years back, but fishing is still a good excuse to go hiking.

There are two ways to find good fishing. The first is to go to someplace nobody knows about. The second is to go someplace that is really difficult to reach. My philosophy is a combination of both. A mountain lake that is too easy to get to will receive heavy pressure, but a lake that is really difficult for people to get to will be the same for you. I recommend choosing a destination that is a little farther than where the common day hike will take you and a little closer than the grueling animal trips of my past. It also depends on the type of fishing you want. If you want challenging fishing for big fish, then a heavily fished lake such as Red Eagle may suit you. If you want to fish where no

In lily pad territory, a raft, wet line, and a leech fly can be an effective combination.

one else is fishing and the fish are easy, try Lake Isabel, one of the park's innermost lakes. See the Vacation Planner for other suggestions.

Some mountain lakes, such as Ole Lake, require little strategy. Others, such as Oldman Lake, can make it hard to bring one in. The ideal strategy for all lakes is to cast to rising fish. If it is an obvious hatch such as an evening mayfly hatch on Elizabeth Lake, fly choice is easy. When the lake is calm and not much is happening on top, I usually try an Adams irresistible or an elk hair caddis, which imitates both a stonefly and a caddis fly.

First, you must figure out where to prospect. Each site description in this book provides suggestions for specific places to fish, but following are some general guidelines for finding fish in mountain lakes:

- If there are no rises, the inlet is usually the best place to fish. Fish, especially in warm weather, like the colder and oxygen-rich water that flows into a lake. This water also carries aquatic insects that get swept off streambeds into the current. Therefore, if you use a fly it should be a dark nymph, and if you use a lure it should have coloration and flash similar to the species of fish living in the lake.
- Some lakes connect up a drainage to another lake that also has fish. This means that fry swept down the stream are easy prey for the lunkers waiting at the lake below. Another good place to look is the outlet, because it is also a corridor for fish travel.
- Fish cruise the shore, especially where the wind creates an eddy—a calm pocket of air—at the end of a point. Here, insects that get knocked down by the wind collect at the edge of the calm area, only to get gulped up by feeding trout.
- On calm, sunny days, whitefish come up to the shallows to feed on surface hatches. Lake trout will often follow them into the shallows,

FLIES AND LURES FOR MOUNTAIN LAKE FISHING

Flies: Adams irresistible, parachute hare's ear, gray Wulff, olive elk hair caddis, olive woolly bugger, orange scud, yellow Marabou muddler, bead-head girdle bug with clipped short rubber legs

Lures: red-and-white Daredevles (small and large sizes), gold and rainbow Thomas Cyclones, fluorescent orange and gold Krocodiles, yellow and black Mepps, large silver spoons (assorted colors) for lake trout fishing

Bait: worms, grasshoppers, corn, marshmallows (Monty says sausage is the way to go for lake trout.) Generally, it is not a good idea to fish with bait in waters inhabited by bull trout; however, bait-fishing is also an effective way to remove lake trout from an aquatic environment in which they may be competing with bull trout. Use your best judgment and a single hook. In the backcountry, bait must be carefully attended and hung on the food pole when not attended, just as any other food or potential bear attractant. *Regulations prohibit collecting bait in the park.*

increasing your chances of catching one near shore. This is especially true in Waterton and Saint Mary Lakes.

PRESENTATION FOR GLACIER'S LAKES

Fly anglers should alternate short and long stripping line for woolly buggers and muddlers, preferably near drop-offs and logjams. For dry flies, get the line out a ways and take a nap. Nymphs are best when floated in an inlet with just a tad of tension on the line. Shrimp should be slowly dragged deep on sinking line.

Lures are pretty simple. Throw them out, let them sink in deep water, and reel them in. Do not reel too fast, and stop occasionally to imitate a resting fish, but be careful not to stop for long; you might lose the lure. Leaving lures in the lake is bad for fish and bad for fishing.

Daypack or Backpack Fishing Equipment

The following is a list of *additional* equipment you would add to your 40–50-pound backpack or 10–15-pound daypack to fish and fish hard in Glacier's backcountry. For more information on lightweight backpacking, pick up a copy of *Backpacking Tips* (Falcon, 1998).

What you could carry
- ❏ Lightweight float tube
- ❏ Gore-Tex waders
- ❏ Lightweight plastic fins
- ❏ Wading shoes
- ❏ Fly rod
- ❏ Fly rod case
- ❏ Fishing vest/fanny pack (fly-fishing equipment)
  - ❏ Fly reel
  - ❏ Dry and wet line spools
  - ❏ Flies in fly box
  - ❏ Silicon floatant
  - ❏ Clippers
  - ❏ Hemostats
  - ❏ Tippet
  - ❏ Spare leaders
  - ❏ Indicator putty
  - ❏ Regulations or fishing license where needed

Or
- ❏ Fishing vest/fanny pack (spin-fishing equipment)
  - ❏ Box of lures
  - ❏ Swivels
  - ❏ Extra line
  - ❏ Needle nose pliers (for disarming treble hooks)
  - ❏ Spin reel
  - ❏ Bait hooks
  - ❏ Worms/power bait (in non-bull trout waters)

What Russ carries
- ❏ Thick cycling tights
- ❏ Neoprene socks
- ❏ Wading shoes or Tevas
- ❏ Three-piece fly rod
- ❏ Walking stick/fly rod case
- ❏ Fanny pack
  - ❏ Fly reel
  - ❏ Dry and wet line spools

- ❏ Flies in fly box
- ❏ Extra flies in small container (in case you drop your flies in the river and they float away)
- ❏ Silicon floatant
- ❏ Clippers
- ❏ Hemostats
- ❏ Tippet
- ❏ Spare leaders (5x and 6x)
- ❏ Indicator putty
- ❏ River map
- ❏ Line cleaning pads
- ❏ Needle nose pliers
- ❏ Montana fishing regulations, Blackfeet fishing regulations, Glacier National Park fishing regulations
- ❏ Tribal fishing license, Montana fishing license, guide license

Other gear Russ brings when appropriate (I rarely carry spin gear unless specifically targeting lake trout.)
- ❏ Spin gear
  - ❏ Spin rod
  - ❏ Spin reel
  - ❏ Box of lures
  - ❏ Swivels
  - ❏ Extra line
- ❏ Two-person Trail Raft
  - ❏ Pump
  - ❏ Life jacket(s)
  - ❏ Paddles

Resident Fish

Glacier National Park supports twenty-six different species of fish, including native westslope cutthroat trout, mountain whitefish, pygmy whitefish, bull trout, and lake trout, the latter native only to the Hudson Bay drainage. The park's waters also hold redside shiner, fathead minnow, burbot, northern pike, and more, as described below. The seven non-native species in the park are Yellowstone cutthroat trout, rainbow trout, brook trout, Kokanee, lake whitefish, arctic grayling, and lake trout, the latter introduced into the Columbia River drainage.

BROOK TROUT (EBT)

Brook trout *(Salvelinus fontinalis)* are uniquely characterized by wormlike markings, dark olive green color, red spots encircled with blue, and white-edged fins. They feed primarily on aquatic insects and prefer small, clear streams with undercut banks and vegetative cover. They tend not to hybridize successfully with other species of trout. Brook trout also are a little more challenging to catch; they are more selective and often stop feeding during midday while hiding in the shadows. They spawn from September to mid-October in shallow gravel beds of streams and lakes. Hybrid brook-bull trout generally are sterile, but some backcrosses do occur.

BULL TROUT (BT)

Many years ago, bull trout *(Salvelinus confluentus)* made fishing in Glacier famous. Today it is the one species that cannot legally be kept or even sought in the park. You may catch one of these fish unintentionally, but you must release it immediately. The U.S. Fish and Wildlife Service listed bull trout in 1998 as a threatened species under the Endangered Species Act. It is hard to say that over-fishing did not have some impact on the bull trout population, but the decline resulted from a number of factors, none of which is directly measurable. These factors include the damming of the South Fork of the Flathead by Hungry Horse Dam in 1953, siltation of streams outside the park from increased logging, and the introduction of rainbow and lake trout into the system. There is no simple answer, but one result is that it is illegal to target (or intentionally fish for) bull trout.

A long body, large mouth, dark green color, light yellow spotting, and a few red to orange spots characterize bull trout. The tail is forked, but not as deeply as the tail of a lake trout. Bull trout are large predatory fish, primarily eating other fish. They traditionally migrated from Flathead Lake in the summer, spawning in shallow tributaries from late September to early November. Bull trout are native to the west side of the Continental Divide and to the Saint Mary River drainage east of the divide.

It is also hard to say when bull trout fishing will open again, but Jack Stanford of the Flathead Lake Biological Research Station stated the status of the Flathead Basin as follows: "Bull trout populations in the Swan and South Fork drainages are healthy, although population segments have seriously declined in Flathead Lake and the North and Middle Forks of the Flathead River. The 1998 bull trout redd counts in these segments are encouraging,

although, for a variety of reasons, it is uncertain if populations can reach former numbers." Recent redd counts continue to show promise, but not too
much promise.

LAKE TROUT (LT)

Lake trout *(Salvelinus namaycush)* are native to the Saint Mary and Waterton
drainages in Glacier National Park. A deeply forked tail identifies them, with
the shortest ray less than one-half the length of the longest ray. The leading
edges of the fins are often white. The body of the fish has numerous light
spots, yellowish to off-white, which also cover the dorsal fin and tail. Lake
trout are sometimes confused with bull trout because both species have forked
tails, but the bull trout lacks the spots found on the lake trout's dorsal fin and
tail, and the bull trout's tail is less forked than that of the lake trout. Bull trout
also often have red spots, although the red spots may be faint in younger fish.
Lake trout were introduced to the Flathead River system on the west side of
the Continental Divide. Lake trout are predatory in nature and feed primarily
on westslope cutthroat, whitefish, rainbow trout, and any other species small
enough to eat. Similar to bull trout in predatory habits, lake trout compete for
the finite amount of forage fish and are generally considered detrimental to
bull trout populations. Lake trout spawn from late October into November in
shallow water near shorelines. They generally inhabit deep water in lakes but
follow prey species into rivers and are commonly caught in both forks of the
Flathead during late summer.

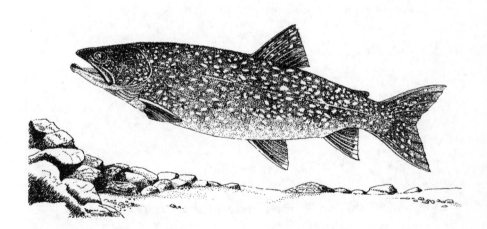

TIPS FOR IDENTIFYING BULL, BROOK, AND LAKE TROUT

It is very important to properly identify any fish you catch. A good guide is your copy of the state fishing regulations, which contain color pictures of the relevant fish. However, fish look different depending on their environment. It is also very important in the Flathead River system, as you should keep both brook and lake trout you catch and release all bull trout. Releasing a lake trout back in the river is almost as bad as taking a bull or cutthroat home and eating it.

TAIL

- Lake trout have a deeply forked tail.
- Bull trout have a slightly forked tail.
- Brook trout have a nearly square tail.

MARKINGS

- Lake trout are consistently patterned across the body, with no red spots, and are almost monochrome patterned; however, lake trout out of Cosley Lake are almost brown colored, whereas lake trout out of Lake McDonald are a nice, calm gray.
- Bull trout have more color variation and usually visible red spots on the sides, mingled with soft pale yellow spots, and have much more of a green tint than lake trout.
- Brook trout: Well, brook trout look like brook trout, but they don't have a forked tail and they do have worm tracks (wavy markings in addition to a dark brown-orange coloration).

PECTORAL FINS

- Lake trout fins meld with the body coloration.
- Bull trout have a white leading edge on their pale green fins.
- Brook trout have a white leading edge, but also a very pronounced black highlight to their pectoral fins, something absent in bull or lake trout.

DORSAL FIN

- The bull trout dorsal has no markings, whereas both brook and lake trout have markings. Commonly referred to as, "No black put it back."
- Brook trout have black spots and squiggles on the dorsal fin.
- Lake trout have black markings on the dorsal fin similar to the monotone coloration of the rest of the body.

ARCTIC GRAYLING (AG)

Arctic grayling *(Thymallus arcticus)* are easily identified by their large and colorful blue dorsal fins. They also have scales similar to those of whitefish, forked tails, and dark spots. Arctic grayling feed vigorously on the surface and live primarily on aquatic insects. Both native and planted populations exist in Montana, but they are not native to Glacier. They spawn in the spring, generally later than rainbow and cutthroat trout.

KOKANEE SALMON (KS)

Kokanee *(Oncorhynchus nerka)* are non-native game fish. This close relative of the sockeye salmon does not venture to sea to spawn. Kokanee were first

stocked in Montana in Flathead Lake but no longer make up a significant population there. In the park they can be found in Swiftcurrent, McDonald, and Bowman Lakes. Kokanee primarily eat plankton and freshwater shrimp. They inhabit cold-water lakes and spawn in the shallows of lakes and streams in November and December. The greenish blue on their dorsal sides and fins, black speckling, and forked tails identify them.

LAKE WHITEFISH (LWF)

Lake whitefish *(Coregonus clupeaformis)* are probably native to Saint Mary Lake and were planted in waters throughout Montana. This species is an important forage species for predatory fish, especially lake trout. Lake whitefish share the same identifying characteristics as mountain whitefish but can be distinguished from that species by a flatter and deeper body shape; mountain whitefish are nearly round in cross-section and tend to be smaller in size. Lake whitefish live primarily in larger, deeper lakes and feed deeper, on zooplankton, and less on aquatic insects than mountain whitefish do. Lake whitefish spawn between October and January in shallow areas of lakes and streams. Interestingly, a major spawning of lake whitefish occurs every fall in the Flathead River above Flathead Lake and has attracted a sizable following of anglers.

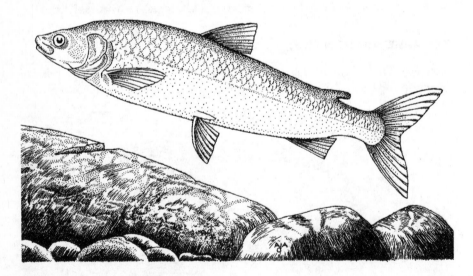

MOUNTAIN WHITEFISH (MWF)

Mountain whitefish *(Prosopium williamson)* are native to both sides of the Continental Divide and are one of the more common fish in the park. They have small mouths and feed primarily on aquatic insects, often rising to dry flies. They feed in mountain lakes, cold streams, and even larger lakes. Mountain whitefish spawn in October and early November in shallow streams.

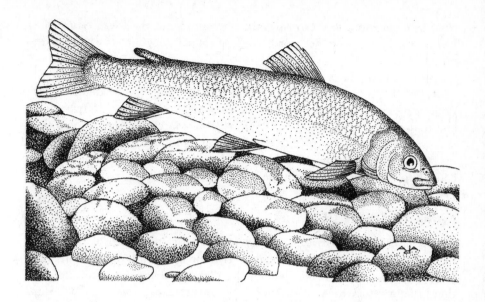

Their small mouths, the presence of large scales (as opposed to the skin on a trout), their forked tails, and as the name suggests, their white color, identify them.

NORTHERN PIKE (NP)

Like my grandpa once joked, "You don't stick your thumb in the mouth of a northern." Northern pike *(Esox lucius)* are good at one thing: eating whatever they can get their teeth on. And they do have teeth. You have a good

chance of catching northerns in Lake Sherburne and the lower Saint Mary River. Often referred to as "northerns" or "pike," they are closely related to pickerel.

Northern pike have long slender bodies and are dark green in color, with white spots, a long flat mouth, a forked tail, and dorsal and anal fins positioned very close to the rear of the fish. They prefer warm-water bays of lakes and the backwaters of rivers. Pike spawn from March through May in shallow areas of lakes or rivers with weeds and grass to hold their eggs. Pike feed on forage fish, small birds, snakes, rodents, and anything else that is small enough to swallow and falls in the water. Watch your toes.

RAINBOW TROUT (RT)

Rainbow trout *(Oncorhyncus mykiss)* are not native to Glacier National Park but were introduced to the Flathead River drainage. Rainbows feed primarily on aquatic insects and reside in cold, clean lakes and streams. They spawn in the spring a little earlier than, but in the same stream habitats as, westslope cutthroat and compete for aquatic insects and other food sources; they also interbreed with the native species and threaten the genetic integrity of pure strains of westslope cutthroat. Rainbows can be distinguished from cutthroat by the lack of "cut" marks on the lower jaw. They have a greenish color with a red midline; the color gradient gives the "rainbow" look. They have dark spots and grow larger than cutthroat trout.

WESTSLOPE CUTTHROAT TROUT (WCT)

Westslope cutthroats *(Oncorhynchus clarki lewisi)* are native to the entire Columbia River drainage west of the Continental Divide and occur in some isolated areas east of the divide. Westslope cutthroats feed primarily on aquatic insects and inhabit cold, clean waters of lakes and streams. They spawn in early spring roughly at the same time as rainbow and Yellowstone cutthroat trout, in gravelly, shallow streams. Like Yellowstone cutthroat, westslope cutthroat have red or "cut" marks on the lower jaw, distinguishing these two species from all other types of fish in Montana. The westslope can be distinguished from the Yellowstone cutthroat by a greener, darker tint and more black spots. They also tend to be rounder, resembling the shape of a rainbow. Because cutthroat often interbreed with rainbows, a common name for a cross between rainbow trout and cutthroat trout has developed: "cutt-bow." Cutt-bows can often be distinguished only by a slight variation in characteristics of either species. Any fish with cut marks should be considered a cutthroat even though it may not be genetically pure.

YELLOWSTONE CUTTHROAT TROUT (YCT)

Yellowstone cutthroat *(Oncorhynchus clarki bouvieri)* are native to the Yellowstone River drainage and are a close relative of the westslope cutthroat. The habits of the Yellowstone cutthroat are similar to those of westslope cutthroat and rainbow trout. Where they occur together, they commonly interbreed. Yellowstone cutthroat trout were stocked in Glacier National Park

lakes before scientists realized that they were genetically distinct from the native westslope cutthroat.

Yellowstone cutthroat can be distinguished from all types of fish except westslope cutthroat by the red or "cut" marks on the lower jaw. They can be distinguished from westslope cutthroat by a more yellow tint and fewer and larger black spots.

SPECIES OF NATIVE AND NONNATIVE FISH IN GLACIER NATIONAL PARK

		Columbia River Drainage	Missouri River Drainage	Hudson Bay Drainage
NATIVE SPECIES				
Salmonids	Westslope cutthroat trout *Oncorhynchus clarki lewisi*	o ♦	o ♦	o ♦
	Bull trout *Salvelinus confluentus*	o ♦		o ♦
	Mountain whitefish *Prosopium williamsoni*	o	o	o
	Pygmy whitefish *Prospium coulteri*	o ♦♦		
	Lake trout *Salvelinus namaycush*			o
Minnows	Redside shiner *Richardsonius balteatus*	o		
	Peamouth *Mylocheilus caurinus*	o		
	Northern squawfish *Ptychocheilus oregonensis*	o		
	Fathead minnow *Pimephales promelas*		o[1]	
Suckers	Longnose sucker *Catostomus catostomus*	o	o	o
	Largescale sucker *Catostomus marcrocheilus*	o		
Sculpins	Slimy sculpin *Cottus cognatus*	o		
	Shorthead sculpin *Cottus confusus*	o ♦		
	Spoonhead sculpin *Cottus ricei*			o ♦
Others	Burbot *Lota lota*			o
	Northern pike *Esox lucius*			o
	Trout perch *Percopsis omiscomaycus*			o ♦♦
NON-NATIVE SPECIES				
Salmonids	Rainbow trout *Oncorhyncus mykiss*	o	o	o
	Brook trout *Salvelinus fontinalis*	o	o	o
	Kokanee Salmon *Oncorhynchus nerka*	o		o
	Yellowstone cutthroat trout *Oncorhynchus clarki bouvieri*	o ♦	o ♦	o ♦
	Lake whitefish *Coregonus clupeaformis*	o[2]		o[2]
	Arctic grayling *Thymallus arcticus*			o ♦
	Lake trout *Salvelinus namaycush*	o ♦♦♦		

Source: Dr. Leo Marnell, National Park Service

o Species present in drainage.
♦ Species of special concern in Montana.
♦♦   Rare in Glacier National Park.
♦♦♦ Non-native in Columbia River Basin. Lake trout are native to the Hudson Bay drainage.

[1] Status of fathead minnow is uncertain. May have been stocked into Three Bears Lake near the Continental Divide on Marias Pass.

[2] Status of lake whitefish is uncertain. Possibly native to Saint Mary Lake in the Hudson Bay drainage.

North Fork of the Flathead River Drainage

1 North Fork of the Flathead River

Location: 11 06 84 577 E 54 30 385 N (Border) 11 07 16 611 E 53 71 973 N (Blankenship)

Length: 58 miles

Species: WCT/A, MWF/A, CBT/C, RT/C-R, BT/C-R, LT/C-R, YCT/R

An angler could spend a week floating the North Fork from the Canadian border to Flathead Lake, but most of us don't have too many weeks to spare and have to settle for a weekend float or an evening wade-fishing the meanders. It is hard to say if the North Fork is underrated or overrated as a fishery. It's overrated if you came to Montana expecting to catch a 5-pound brown trout on your first fly-fishing trip. It's underrated if you've never experienced a truly wild native fishery.

The mystery of the North Fork, and the Middle Fork for that matter, is when and what type of fish you will catch on a given stretch of river. Biologists and anglers alike realize that the North Fork benefits from the lakes connected to it, especially Flathead Lake. Fish that migrate upstream from Flathead Lake help make it possible to catch big fish in the river.

After fishing most of the river and at random enough times, I am convinced that you should be able to catch whitefish, a few rainbows, and smaller cutthroat in the river year-round. However, it may be a lot of hard fishing for a meager fare from November to May.

In the summer the primary fare is cutthroats between 8 and 13 inches long. You can also catch larger cutthroat and rainbows up to 20 inches long. Lure and woolly bugger sluggers may have a chance at some larger migrant lake trout. Make sure to carefully identify your catch and don't release any lake or brook trout caught back into the river system.

For flies I recommend bead-head hare's ear, bead-head Whitlock squirrel nymph, parachute Adams, yellow humpy, sofa pillow, olive woolly bugger, and pink egg sucking leech for muddy water. In the morning, a parachute Adams fished in a shallow riffle can be deadly. On a hot afternoon, prospecting with a hopper or yellow stimulator is always a good idea. In the fall watch for late-season October caddis and switch to non-standard green stimulators, which are usually better for big caddis than the elk hair or bucktail varieties.

If you try a spoon, I recommend a yellow Panther Martin, a black or red Daredevle, or a silver-and-red Mepps with two hooks removed to facilitate the release of cutthroat and bull trout. Avoid larger lures. Bait-fishing is not recommended; the bull trout's propensity to swallow hooks deep prevents releasing. If you do catch a bull and are unable to get the hook out without harming the fish, cut the line and leave in the lure. Sometimes a fish has a chance of working the lure free on its own.

The North Fork receives heavy floater use, although there are more canoes and light crafts than rafts and dories. The area gets less outfitter use because of the bumpy, dirt access road. Wade-fishing is concentrated around bridges and campgrounds, especially near Big Creek Campground and the Camas Bridge.

Access from West Glacier: Drive into the park, past the entrance, and follow Going-to-the-Sun Road to a T-junction. At the T-junction on Camas Road, turn left toward Apgar Village and continue straight past several turnoffs to Apgar Village and Fish Creek, heading north on Camas Road. About 15 miles later cross the North Fork on the Camas Bridge. This is the end of good pavement. From here you can drive upstream or downstream along North Fork Road. On the west side of the Camas Bridge is a jeep trail where you can drag a raft or carry a canoe to the river.

Access from North of the Camas Bridge: Drive 3.2 miles north to a pull-out on the right, just before Coal Creek. This is the Coal Creek River Access. You can sometimes back in a trailer, but not at high water. Reach the next access site by driving 1.5 miles to the north, turning right, and driving east through Polebridge for 2 miles to Polebridge River Access. Before crossing the North Fork into the park, there is a well-maintained access site. If you do not stop at Polebridge, continue north on the North Fork Road for 7.5 miles to Ford Work Center, which provides a tricky access point where you will have to drag your raft down to the water.

Big Creek Campground, 2.25 miles south of the Camas Bridge on the Outside North Fork Road, has a rocky but usable boat ramp. At Fool Hen Flats, 3.2 miles south of Big Creek, you can launch a canoe or raft but not a dory; there is no boat ramp. Glacier Rim access, 9.2 miles south of Big Creek on the Outside North Fork Road, is sandy and a little tricky for trailers but heavily used.

The southernmost access site on the North Fork is at Blankenship Bridge, where the river enters the Middle Fork. It is a good access site, but remember to start rowing across the Middle Fork before you pass under the bridge. If you don't pull hard to the south shore at high water, you could miss it.

You can also access the North Fork via the Inside North Fork Road. Turn right off Camas Road about 0.5 mile after crossing McDonald Creek. Take a left as you near Fish Creek Campground. You will not see the river much, but the ride is primitive and wild. I recommend taking a four-wheel-drive vehicle because it is bumpy. Just past Logging Creek you can see the river. Park, bush-whack, and fish. There are no boat ramps on the park side of the river.

You can reach the Outside North Fork Road directly from Columbia Falls. It is 30 miles from West Glacier to Polebridge River Access (28 to Polebridge) and 38 miles from Columbia Falls to Polebridge River Access.

North Fork of the Flathead River Drainage

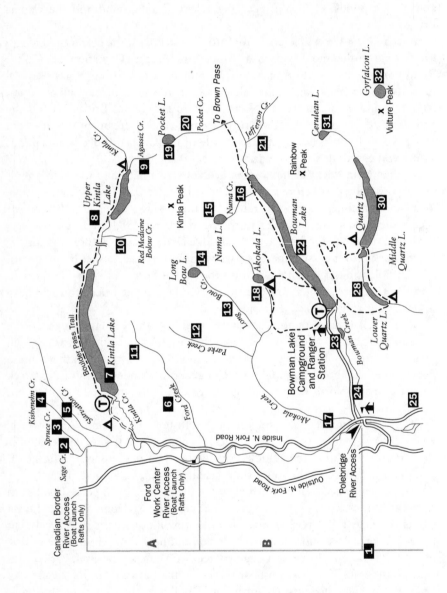

North Fork of the Flathead River Drainage

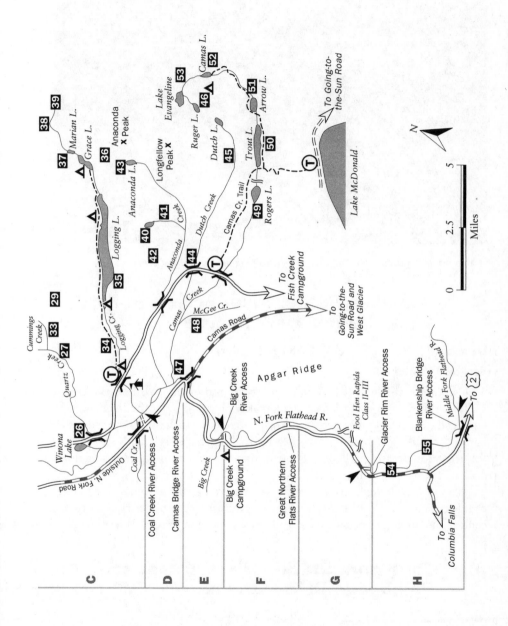

Large boulders and channel choices greet floaters above Glacier Rim.

A. Canadian Border River Access to Ford Work Station River Access

Location: 11 06 84 577 E 54 30 385 N (Border)

Length: 14 miles

This section is the least fished and wildest section of the North Fork. When we float this section, we often send a kayaker ahead to scout the river for log-jams and dangerous "sweepers" (a downed tree or branch obtruding from the bank), both of which can prove deadly to floaters. Check with the Forest Service before floating. This is a good section to fish wet or with lures such as a small Thomas Cyclone.

When I last floated this section, I was amazed at the abundance of large caddis casings on the average overturned river rock. The upper river at times can remind an angler of an extra-productive Montana prairie fishery.

B. Ford Work Station River Access to Polebridge River Access

Location: 11 06 92 611 E 54 06 571 N (Ford)

Length: 11 miles

The major change as you float downstream from Ford is more floaters. It is common to float Ford to Polebridge but rare to float Border to Ford. Less water and bumpier road make the difference. The river passes Round Prairie, as the Park Service likes to call the sagebrush flats on the park side. Round Prairie is a good place for terrestrial imitations. Try an Adams irresistible; its bulky body imitates a mayfly, caddis casing, and several terrestrials, such as beetles and ants. Deep pools can produce plenty of whitefish if you can get your nymph down.

C.   Polebridge River Access to Coal Creek River Access

Location: 11 06 99 749 E 54 06 571 N (Polebridge)

Length: 9 miles

This section also meanders, with rocky bottoms and possible logjams. Spring Creek and Hay Creek enter the river along this stretch. It is a short float to the Coal Creek access; watch for it just after Coal Creek and across from Logging Creek. Fishing is primarily smaller cutthroat with occasional larger fish moving through in early and late summer.

D.   Coal Creek River Access to the Camas Bridge (No Boat Ramp)

Location: 11 07 06 531 E 53 96 551 N (Coal Creek)

Length: 6 miles

Floaters from Coal to Camas or Coal to Big Creek should be wary of channel changes in this section. It is some of the most unpredictable water on the river. In 1995 it was completely blocked by a spring logjam, and several floaters who didn't scout ahead or check with the Forest Service were seriously injured because of this. In 2000, several anglers tried to row a drift boat through here during high water (not advised) and stuck their craft into the logjam, having to be rescued by helicopter from the park side, hypothermic and lucky. The river is different every year sometimes forming large side channels that you should fish as you would a small river. Often, stopping and walking across an island to fish a nice hole on the other side can be very rewarding. This section also contains some of the bigger rainbows and hybrids, which go for parachute hoppers and yellow Sallies late in the summer. *Coal Creek is closed to fishing to facilitate the recovery of bull trout. No fishing is allowed within a 100-yard radius of the mouth of Coal Creek. Check current regulations.*

From Coal Creek River Access to the Camas Bridge, side channels can be productive, but scout ahead for logjams.

E. Camas Bridge (No Boat Ramp) to Big Creek River Access

Location: 11 07 10 892 E 53 89 015 N (Camas)

Length: 3 miles

This section is a good place to try a little lure-fishing. The long, flat runs after the bridge hold some big fish, and they are not always feeding on the surface. There is a little bit of a rock garden just before Big Creek. Try it, and remember to fish the holes on the east side of the river past Big Creek that the campers cannot reach. It also is a good idea to get out of the boat and prospect from shore; some nice holes deserve thorough attention. *Big Creek is closed to fishing to facilitate the recovery of bull trout. No fishing is allowed within a 100-yard radius of the mouth of Big Creek. Check current regulations.*

F. Big Creek River Access to Great Northern Flats River Access

Location: 11 07 11 898 E 53 86 808 N (Big Creek)

Length: 3 miles

This section fishes better but isn't as pretty as the canyon downriver, but it can also get fished pretty hard by float and wade anglers. This makes a nice half-day trip if you can take out with a raft at Great Northern Flats. However, if you prefer a dory and don't like to winch yours across the rocks like a Lavro promotional video, you'd better float downstream to Glacier Rim.

G. Great Northern Flats River Access to Glacier Rim River Access

Location: 11 07 11 898 E 53 83 371 N (Great Northern Flats)

Length: 8 miles

This section is popular with local residents and gets more pressure than upstream reaches. However, it makes a long day if you want to fish it right. It does hold fish, especially in the canyon area, where most attractor patterns should do the trick if the fish are biting. Fishing a nymph can be difficult because of the swirling water, but you can pick up larger fish and give the mouths of the baby cutthroat a rest. Remember, there are upper and lower Fools Hen Rapids; this ain't all easy water. For lures, try a yellow rooster tail, a Panther Martin, or a rainbow Krocodile. Sometimes these waters see a lot of flies and a lure angler can do well. Just remember to disarm your treble hook.

H. Glacier Rim River Access to Blankenship Bridge River Access

Location: 11 07 12 424 E 53 74 819 N (Glacier Rim) 11 07 16 611 E 53 71 973 N (Blankenship)

Length: 4 miles

I float this section a lot and like it, but it isn't as pretty as West Glacier to Blankenship on the Middle Fork or Big Creek to Glacier Rim. It does offer some challenging spring creek–style fishing of clear runs with finicky rainbows. You may need to pull out the small stuff and do some delicate nymphing to be successful on this stretch. The action may be slow, but when you catch one, it will be big. Concentrate especially on the long, flat boulder runs, a favorite of rainbows. During low water, just before Blankenship Bridge you start picking up whitefish on dries. There are some good-sized whitefish and lake trout where the two rivers meet.

Glacier Rim to Blankenship tends to hold more rainbows than other stretches of the river, and that may not be a coincidence. A former commercial hatchery at Sekokini Springs (often confused with Kokanee Springs, but it had nothing to do with the Kokanee Hatchery now owned by MTFWP) may have leaked rainbow trout into this section. However, the hatchery may be renovated to produce genetically pure westslope someday.

2 Sage Creek

Location: 11 06 86 301 E 54 29 057 N

Length: 1.3 miles

Species: WCT/C

From the Canadian border this is the first noticeable tributary of the North Fork of the Flathead on the park side.

3 Spruce Creek

Location: 11 06 88 526 E 54 26 281 N

Length: 3.6 miles

Species: BT/C, WCT/C

4 Kishenehn Creek

Location: 11 06 89 634 E 54 24 987 N

Length: 5.2 miles

Species: WCT/C, BT/R

Blankenship Bridge, the end of many magical days and the beginning of even more.

5 Starvation Creek

Location: 11 06 90 960 E 54 23 372 N
Length: 6.7 miles
Species: WCT/C, BT/R

6 Kintla Creek

Location: 11 06 92 449 E 54 21 074 N
Length: 9.6 miles
Species: WCT/C, BT/C

From Kintla Lake until Kintla Creek pours into the North Fork of the Flathead River, this western trout stream has long been marked by natural beauty. The stream provides important rearing habitat for juvenile cutthroat that later populate the main river. If you decide to stop and fish this a bit on your way to Kintla Lake, I suggest a 3-weight fly rod and a few bushy barbless stimulators. *Kintla Creek is closed to fishing above Kintla Lake to facilitate the recovery of bull trout in Kintla Lake.*

7 Kintla Lake

Location: 11 06 94 526 E 54 23 458 N
Elevation: 4,008 ft
Area: 1,728 acres
Species: MWF/A, LT/C, WCT/C, BT/R, KS/R

Fishing along the shores of Kintla Lake can produce some good-sized cutthroat and whitefish. You can also make this a canoe-and-fish trip by paddling your gear to the head of the lake after obtaining a permit to stay there.

The lake can get very still, and when it does the action slows, especially on flies. Find a nice place to sit and wait for a shore-cruising trout, then let a #14 parachute Adams float on top. From a float tube or a canoe, trolling a leech on sinking line can also be effective. Near submerged logs, try fishing a muddler. For lures, consider throwing on a red or gold Mepps for a little more action. Trolling from a canoe with a large silver spoon is also effective for Kokanee and lake trout.

Fishing is best for lake trout in the fall. Access Kintla Lake by driving from Polebridge into the park. Turn left (north) after crossing the North Fork. Drive 15 miles on the Inside North Fork Road to Kintla. Give yourself at least an hour from Polebridge. Kintla Lake receives relatively light fishing pressure; maybe one of ten campers at the head of the lake fishes, the rest are primarily hikers. The lake does get heavier fishing pressure toward the foot, but the

The view of Kinnerly from the campground at the head of Kintla Lake.

long, bumpy drive to the lake prevents most people from visiting it. *Motorized boats are not allowed on Kintla Lake.*

8 Upper Kintla Lake

Location: 11 07 04 601 E 54 28 232 N
Elevation: 4,371 ft
Area: 460 acres
Species: BT/C

Upper Kintla Lake is closed to fishing to protect the genetically unique population of bull trout that inhabit the lake. A wise man once told me another unique aspect of Upper Kintla Lake: The wind causes the lake to oscillate or rock, swelling the waterline alternately at each end of the lake. Take a nap at the foot of the lake sometime in the sun and watch the waterline. Also, some very interesting large insects hatch on the lake, but even when the big bugs are hatching, these bull trout rarely feed on the surface. *Closed to fishing. Check current regulations.*

9 Agassiz Creek

Location: 11 07 08 886 E 54 28 229 N

Length: N/A

Species: possibly juvenile BT/R

Closed to fishing. Check current regulations.

10 Red Medicine Bow Creek

Location: 11 07 03 601 E 54 28 231 N

Length: N/A

Species: possibly juvenile BT/R

Closed to fishing. Check current regulations.

11 Ford Creek

Location: 11 06 93 580 E 54 16 529 N

Length: 8.1 miles

Species: WCT/C, BT/R

Ford Creek, for which the Ford Work Station and River Access are named, is typical of North Fork tributaries: relatively small, good rearing habitat, but not much for the experienced fly-fisher.

12 Parke Creek

Location: 11 07 00 598 E 54 15 655 N

Length: 4.8 miles

Species: WCT/R, BT/R

This little-known tributary of Akokala Creek would be an awful lot of bushwhacking for not an awful lot of big fish, but Parke Creek is an important part of the Akokala ecosystem.

13 Long Bow Creek

Location: 11 07 02 117 E 54 15 650 N

Length: 4.3 miles

Species: WCT/A, BT/C, MWF/C

This small tributary of Akokala Creek may harbor a few small cutthroats.

14 Long Bow Lake

15 Numa Lake

16 Numa Creek

Location: 11 07 11 636 E 54 20 534 N

Length: N/A

Species: WCT/R

Numa Creek runs right through the backcountry campground at the head of Bowman Lake, but it doesn't harbor much in the way of fish. Try Bowman Lake instead.

17 Akokala Creek

Location: 11 06 99 493 E 54 07 152 N

Length: 13.6 miles

Species: WCT/C, BT/R

18 Akokala Lake

Location: 11 07 05 416 E 54 17 137 N

Elevation: 4,735 ft

Area: 24 acres

Species: WCT/C, BT/R

Akokala Lake makes a nice late June or late September day trip, if you like to get some exercise and catch a few fish. The campsite is at the outlet with not much of a view but a nice lakeshore nearby. In the summer the lake can warm up quite a bit in the day, and fish tend to move to the deeper south shore and toward the cool water of the inlet. The best fishing is in the early morning and evening, true of most mountain lakes, but especially with the more accessible areas of this lake being shallow and less likely to hold fish during midday. I recommend wading across the outlet and fishing the south shore around to the inlet or, for overnight visitors, making a loop around the lake. A #14 Adams irresistible or #12 Prince nymph or your favorite single-hook lure should take a few fish after you locate them. Fishing can be slow if you don't see rising fish in your area.

The lake gets relatively light hiker and angler use due to no extended trip options, but this could be a nice two-day overnight. Bring your two-person raft. If you're wondering, it really isn't feasible to hike to Numa Lookout from the lake, unless you like scratched legs and a really steep, thick bushwhack. Access the lookout by hiking 5.8 miles from the north side of the Bowman Lake Campground loop on the Akokala Lake Trail.

Fishing the outlet of Akokala Lake. KIM SCHNEIDER PHOTO

19 Pocket Lake

Although the lake is fishless, the hike from the Boulder Pass Trail up Boulder Peak is worth it for a view of the lake.

20 Pocket Creek

Location: 11 07 14 030 E 54 23 997 N

Length: N/A

Species: WCT/A, BT/C, MWF/C

Closed to fishing. Check current regulations.

21 Jefferson Creek

Location: 11 07 12 927 E 54 21 667 N

Length: N/A

Species: WCT/A, BT/C, MWF/C

Closed to fishing. Check current regulations.

22 Bowman Lake

Location: 11 07 05 828 E 54 11 936 N

Elevation: 4,030 ft

Area: 1,735 acres

Species: MWF/C, LT/C, WCT/C, BT/R, KS/R

Bowman has never been on the top of my list. It does contain fish, and the head of the lake may be very productive, but the head is usually closed for eagle nesting. The foot and the outlet look very attractive and sometimes produce fish, but your best bet is fishing from the campground near the head of the lake, where a little inlet flows in. If you have a boat, try trolling in the middle or fishing the north shore. To fish for Kokanee and lake trout, troll with cowbells, Ford fenders, and cherry bobbers. For flies, a gray Wulff should be good enough for a few strikes. A soft-hackle hare's ear or pheasant tail fished on dry line to rising fish is also effective. If you get away from the foot of the lake, a woolly bugger on wet line should produce a few fish. A large silver spoon fished deep is also effective.

The heaviest use happens near the foot, where vehicle access and boat ramps allow for boats with ten or less horsepower motors. You can reach Bowman Lake from Polebridge by crossing into the park and turning north (left), then turning right (east) for a bumpy, primitive drive to Bowman Lake Campground, at the foot of the lake (total distance from park entrance: 6

A shot across the bow, fall fishing on Bowman Lake.

miles). There are trails heading south and north along the edge of the lake and a boat ramp. The southern trail to Quartz Lake allows access to the outlet in 0.4 mile but does not offer access to the shoreline much farther after that. The trail on the north shore passes the ranger station and follows the lake to the designated campsite close to the head of the lake. Several large boulders along the trail make good fishing rest stops. At the campground at the head of Bowman Lake, you can fish right from camp.

23 Unnamed Lake (Lower Bowman)

Location: 11 07 04 977 E 54 11 025 N
Area: N/A
Species: WCT/C, BT/R, MWF/R

24 Bowman Creek

Location: 11 06 99 725 E 54 06 727 N
Length: 12.7 miles
Species: WCT/C, BT/R, MWF/R

Like most North Fork tributaries, Bowman Creek holds a few small and mid-sized cutthroats, but it is primarily spawning and rearing habitat. However, the creek is easily accessed along the drive to Bowman Lake from Polebridge and can make for a pleasant break from the bumpy ride. *Closed to fishing above Bowman Lake. Check current regulations.*

25 Hidden Meadow Ponds

26 Winona Lake

Location: 11 07 03 440 E 54 00 430 N

Elevation: 3,492 ft

Area: 49 acres

Species: WCT/C

The fishing in Winona Lake is a lot like the fishing in Howe Lakes, which, although they do not drain into the North Fork, are in the same geographic area. However, Winona Lake is a lot bigger lake than it looks on the map and has potential for a few larger cutthroats. It is tough to even get a good picture of this boggy lake without some type of raft or canoe. Generally, the fish are relatively small but fun to catch. Use a woolly worm or leech fly or try brighter lures. Located just north of Quartz Creek on the Inside North Fork Road, it gets moderate use because of the easy access, but the lake is not known for great fishing, so you may have it to yourself. I suggest fishing early or late in the season when the water is cool. On hot summer days fishing is slow and fish are sluggish.

To get to the lake, drive 3.3 miles south of the Polebridge entrance station on the Inside North Fork Road. Winona Lake is on your right (to the west), next to the road 0.5 mile north of Quartz Creek.

27 Quartz Creek

Location: 11 07 04 242 E 53 99 265 N

Length: 13.7 miles

Species: WCT/A, BT/C, MWF/C

28 Lower Quartz Lake

Location: 11 07 07 707 E 54 08 600 N

Elevation: 4,191 ft

Area: 171 acres

Species: WCT/A, MWF/C, BT/C

Fishing for small cutthroat at the outlet is usually productive, although this section gets fished the most. Wade out in the lake and fish the evening hatch. This is the only easily accessible place to fish without a float tube or boat.

However, the trail continues up the southern shore and you can get to the water by a steep, thick bushwhack. The areas away from the outlet get far less pressure and offer more solitude and bigger fish. For even bigger fish, consider trolling from a float tube or rubber raft. A small red Daredevle is usually productive, especially in deeper areas of the lake. There is heavy hiker and angler use at the outlet, where the campground is located, but few people bushwhack to the inlet. From the foot of Bowman Lake, hike over Quartz Ridge on the Lower Quartz Lake Trail for 3.5 miles to the campground at the foot of the lake.

29 Middle Quartz Lake

Location: 11 07 09 527 E 54 11 549 N

Elevation: 4,397 ft

Area: 51 acres

Species: WCT/C, BT/C, MWF/C

Fishing the inlet is the most common way to bring a cutthroat out of Middle Quartz, but consider evening fishing off the steep banks to the north of the inlet. A muddler or woolly worm fished in the inlet or a small humpy can be productive. For nymphing I would try a small pheasant tail tied several feet past an indicator fly on a two-fly rig. From the foot of Bowman Lake, hike 6.4 miles over Quartz Ridge on Quartz Lake Trail and continue for less than a mile to where a log bridge crosses Quartz Creek. You can follow either side of the creek down to the inlet.

30 Quartz Lake

Location: 11 07 10 369 E 54 11 232 N

Elevation: 4,416 ft

Area: 882 acres

Species: WCT/A, MWF/C, BT/C

The action at Quartz Lake can be quite steady, and I rate it much better fishing than Bowman Lake, even though much less shoreline of Quartz Lake is accessible. A float tube or raft is worth the extra weight here. The best places to fish Quartz are also the most commonly fished. The logjam probably gets the most pressure but also produces many fish, especially small cutthroat. Cruising fish will rise here even when there are few rises on the lake.

A red or yellow humpy or stimulator or female Adams is a good fly for surface feeders. Also try a yellow Marabou muddler fished wet. For lures, Thomas Cyclone and red-and-gold Mepps have proven very effective, but remember to cut off two of the treble hooks before lure-fishing.

The lake receives a lot of hiker visitation and some angler use at the foot. It is accessible from the foot of Bowman Lake by hiking 6.4 miles on Quartz Lake Trail over Cerulean Ridge to the foot of Quartz Lake. It is a gentle but long climb in, and carrying any type of raft demands excellent physical conditioning for the 1,400-foot climb.

31 Cerulean Lake

Location: 11 07 16 178 E 54 16 859 N

Elevation: 4,733 ft

Area: 52 acres

Species: WCT/A, BT/C

Cerulean Lake is one of the highest lakes in the park. It is inhabited by indigenous fish and cutthroat and is rarely fished. Many backcountry travelers spend more of their time getting to this lake than fishing it. Monty Parratt once led me to Cerulean after a grueling 7:00 A.M. departure from Bowman and arrived back at Bowman at 10:40 P.M. I had three casts, caught one small cutthroat on a little parachute Adams, and bushwhacked out. Despite the difficult trip, the view toward Rainbow Glacier was spectacular. Most common dries should work since the lake receives few anglers, but you should try to work your way around the east side, across the logjam, for better casting. Be careful of bears. This is definitely a lake for catch-and-release fishing.

Use is light and there is very difficult, regulated access. The only time to fish this lake is on a sunny late-summer day. There is no trail to Cerulean Lake, but it is somewhat accessible from the nearest trailhead at the foot of Bowman Lake. Carry your raft over Cerulean Ridge on Quartz Lake Trail from the foot of Bowman Lake, then paddle the 4 miles to the east end of Quartz Lake. The route from here to the foot of Cerulean is a 1.5-mile bushwhack through some of the densest and most heavily populated grizzly habitat in Glacier. The trip can make for a very long day or, more realistically, two days. Because there is no campsite at Cerulean Lake, most people do not get to this lake.

32 Gyrfalcon Lake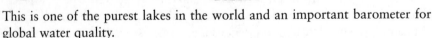

This is one of the purest lakes in the world and an important barometer for global water quality.

33 Cummings Creek

Location: 11 07 08 095 E 54 04 680 N

Length: 7.2 miles

The hardy angler will be rewarded at Cerulean Lake. DALE AYOTTE PHOTO

Species: WCT/C, BT/R, MWF/R

This tributary of Quartz Creek can be accessed from Quartz Creek Trail with a GPS or good route-finding skills.

34 Logging Creek

Location: 11 07 06 525 E 53 96 715 N

Length: 10.5 miles

Species: WCT/C, BT/R, MWF/R

Closed to fishing between Logging Lake and Grace Lake. Check current regulations. Below Logging Lake, the creek offers a few smaller cutthroats.

35 Logging Lake

Location: 11 07 10 558 E 54 01 755 N

Elevation: 3,810 ft

Area: 1,136 acres

Species: MWF/C, LT/C, WCT/C, BT/C

Logging Lake is not the most productive of lakes in the North Fork, but it does contain large lake and bull trout that feed on smaller whitefish and cutthroats. The two campgrounds on the lake provide the majority of fishing opportunities. The campground at the foot of Logging Lake is in mucky country and makes fishing from shore difficult. Adair Campground, a backcountry site near the head of the lake, has a little inlet that is good for fly-fishing for small whitefish. Bring a float tube to get to deeper water. The lake is generally pretty shallow near shore and even the inlet is very flat, offering little shelf habitat. Small mayfly patterns should take a few cutthroat and whitefish.

Many hikers in this area are also anglers, because you do not visit Logging Lake for spectacular scenery. Grace Lake is well known for its fishing, and anglers headed that way often fish Logging Lake from the foot or from the Adair Backcountry Campground toward the head of the lake. There are four sites at each of the lake's two campgrounds that allow for a maximum of thirty-two campers around the lake at one time. These campgrounds do not fill up often, except at peak season. This is a good early-season, low-elevation fishing trip.

Getting to the lake requires making a 20-mile drive on the primitive Inside North Fork Road from Fish Creek Campground to the Logging Creek Ranger Station and Trailhead. You can also take the Outside North Fork Road through Polebridge, which cuts your primitive road driving on the Inside Road to about 7 miles, but either way it is a dirt road drive. It is 4.4 miles on Logging Lake Trail to the foot of Logging Lake and 10 miles to the head. The first part of the trail crosses through an old burn, but the rest of the trail is relatively flat and in the trees. Although the trail follows the lake, you can only see the water in a couple of places, and access to the shore is limited.

36 Grace Lake

Location: 11 07 20 309 E 54 07 721 N

Elevation: 3,920 ft

Area: 62 acres

Species: WCT-YCT Hybrids/C

Grace Lake has nice-sized cutthroat, generally 14 to 16 inches long, sometimes bigger. The best fishing is at the inlet, but it is common to catch fish by the backcountry campground near the foot of the lake. The wind can make fly-fishing difficult, but a slight breeze makes it harder for fish to detect artificial flies. There is no trail around the lake, but it is a short 0.5-mile bushwhack to the inlet. If you spend a couple of nights at Grace, I suggest bushwhacking up the drainage a bit for equally productive fishing in the upper lake, Marian Lake, which is less fished than Grace. A Zug bug fished wet in the inlet is deadly, although you may not have to work that hard. An elk hair caddis or Adams irresistible should take fish on the surface. If it is windy, try a yellow Marabou muddler or spin fish with a yellow rooster tail.

There is fairly light hiker use but relatively heavy angler use from the Adair Backcountry Campground (four sites) and the Grace Lake Backcountry Campground (three sites). Most fishing pressure is concentrated at the campground near the outlet and just up the north shore. Grace Lake is 12.8 miles from Logging Creek Ranger Station on the Logging Lake Trail.

37 Marian Lake

Location: 12 02 80 129 E 54 09 240 N

Elevation: 3,946 ft

Area: N/A

Species: WCT-YCT Hybrids/C

This lake just above Grace Lake, commonly referred to as Marian Lake, has fishing similar to Grace, although it receives less pressure and is harder to reach. An Adams irresistible should take fish. From Logging Creek Ranger Station, hike 12.8 miles to Grace Lake, bushwhack around the lake to the inlet, and fish up the stream through a nasty little bushwhack for less than a mile to Marian Lake.

38 Unnamed Lake (Above Marian Lake)

Location: 12 02 80 526 E 54 10 524N

Elevation: 4,170 ft

Area: N/A

Species: WCT-YCT Hybrids/C

39 Unnamed Lake (Below Trapper Peak)

40 Unnamed Lake (Adair Pond)

If there are fish in this small lake near the old Logging Fire Lookout, they're safe.

41 Unnamed Lake (Anaconda Pond)

42 Anaconda Creek

Location: 11 07 10 368 E 53 90 536 N

Length: 15.7 miles

Species: WCT/C, BT/R, MWF/R

The creek is populated with smaller cutthroat trout up to 11 miles up from the mouth, where a falls blocks upstream migration. This is important rearing habitat for trout destined for the North Fork of the Flathead River.

43 Anaconda Lake

The lake may have been stocked at one time but is not known to support fish.

44 Dutch Creek

Location: 11 07 13 683 E 53 90 617 N

Length: 11.3 miles

Species: WCT/C, BT/R, MWF/R

Dutch Creek can be very small in places and doesn't hold many fish. It is best fished near where it enters Camas Creek.

45 Dutch Lakes

All three lakes are fishless, although the main lake was planted in the past. Dutch Lakes really don't have much in the way of viable spawning habitat, as the creek drops steeply shortly after exiting the lakes and there is no gravelly inlet. This is a good place for grizzlies.

46 Ruger Lake

We wondered if Ruger Lake would have fish, and I actually put a fly in it, but I don't think it had any fish. There were no signs of fish and none of the literature indicates that there are fish here.

47 Camas Creek

Location: 11 07 10 668 E 53 90 065 N
Length: 18.8 miles

Lower Camas Creek spreads across its floodplain.

Species: WCT/C, BT/R, MWF/R, RBT/R

Camas Creek is full of cutthroat in places near the lakes but doesn't hold many large fish year-round. The lower section spreads out in the floodplain and is best left unfished until fall. Camas Creek is reached via a short, bumpy drive on the Inside North Fork Road north of Fish Creek Campground.

48 McGee Creek

Location: 11 07 15 171 E 53 90 369 N

Length: N/A

Species: WCT/A, BT/C, MWF/C

Closed to fishing. Check current regulations.

49 Rogers Lake

Location: 12 02 83 152 E 53 93 260 N

Elevation: 3,793 ft

Area: 87 acres

Species: WCT/R, BT/R, MWF/R

The lake is shallow and offers slow fishing for small cutthroats. The canyon between the bridge across Camas Creek and the inlet of Rogers Lake is a wild and scenic land, more mystical than the lake. Fish during midsummer when trout from the North Fork of the Flathead or those that have been washed down the cascades from Trout Lake might be taken in the lake. A red Daredevle should do the trick, but a pheasant tail fished off the inlet shelf should get the more finicky fish.

Turn north off Going-to-the-Sun Road at the head of Lake McDonald and drive around the head of the lake for 0.5 mile to the Trout Lake Trailhead. Hike 3.7 miles over Howe Ridge on the Trout Lake Trail. Upon reaching the junction with the Camas Creek Trail, turn left and walk to the bridge over Camas Creek. Follow the north side of the canyon down to the lake.

50 Trout Lake

Location: 12 02 84 741 E 53 94 595 N

Elevation: 3,903 ft

Area: 225 acres

Species: WCT/A, BT/C, WCT-YCT Hybrids/R

Trout Lake is probably more infamous for bear maulings than for trophy trout due to the 1967 Night of the Grizzly incident that closed the campground at the foot of the lake. (It was still closed as of this printing and there are no known plans for reopening the campground.) It does, however, offer fishing for larger-than-average cutthroats. The easiest way to fish this lake is to make a day trip out of it. Start early for more fishing and remember that the climb over Howe Ridge is not for wimps. The easiest and most popular place to fish is at the foot of the lake on the logjam. Here small cutthroat are commonly taken on flies and bigger fish on lures, although it can be slow during midday. A rainbow Mepps is a good lure here.

Hike 3.5 miles from the Trout Lake Trailhead over Howe Ridge on the Trout Lake Trail to the foot of Trout Lake, which is fairly open and offers plenty of casting room off the logjam. You can also hike farther up the lake and bushwhack down almost anyplace, but remember your time constraints if you are day hiking. Most of the avalanche chutes and the rocks near the inlet are too far for most day-trippers. The head of the lake does have some comfortable rocks to roost on.

51 Arrow Lake

Location: 12 02 87 643 E 53 98 256 N

Elevation: 4,070 ft

Area: 59 acres

Species: WCT-YCT Hybrids/C, BT/R, MWF/R

Veteran West Glacier angler Ev Lundgren has fond memories of fishing Arrow Lake and staying at a cabin here. Nowadays the cabin is gone, you can't have a fire anymore, and you can stay only at the backcountry campground at the foot of the lake. The fish in this lake are cagey, and lures probably take more fish than flies. The talus slope on the south shore also is a good spot, with plenty of backcast room and deep water.

The fishing shuts off during midday, and it is worth your while to get up early. The lakes above Arrow contain healthy populations of Yellowstone cutthroat, and you are wise to fish a muddler in the inlet. Fish the big rocks on the south shore, watching for cruising fish. If you cannot quite get your fly out far enough, try a bobber and fly rig.

Access is by hiking 7 miles over Howe Ridge from the Trout Lake Trailhead at the head of Lake McDonald. This is no day hike.

52 Camas Lake

Location: 12 02 88 042 E 54 02 160 N

Elevation: 5,076 ft

Area: 20 acres

Species: YCT/C

A typical Yellowstone cutthroat trout taken from Lake Evangeline.

The fishing here is not as good as at Arrow or Evangeline. The campground has two sites and seems very private. The best fishing is on the far, east shore. The inlet is very boggy. In fact, it is boggy all the way to Evangeline. Use a yellow humpy and bitch creek nymph fished deep and wet on sinking line. The lake gets light use because of the distance from the trailhead; there are only two campsites.

Hike 13.8 miles over Howe Ridge from the Trout Lake Trailhead on the Trout Lake Trail. The section from Arrow Lake to Camas is the toughest, full of thick brush.

53 Lake Evangeline

Location: 12 02 86 441 E 54 03 617 N

Elevation: 5,247 ft

Area: 70 acres

Species: YCT/C

I have been to Lake Evangeline twice. The first time we caught a fish on every cast. The next time, loons were on the lake and we had to work a little for the fish. A yellow Marabou muddler or Panther Martin should do the trick. If the fishing is tough, try a mosquito fished wet in one of the misty inlets. Hike 13.9 miles on the Trout Lake Trail from the Trout Lake Trailhead over Howe

Ridge and all the way up the Camas Valley to Camas Lake. Camp there two nights and bushwhack 1.5 miles to Evangeline.

54 Unnamed Ponds (Glacier Rim Area)

These three or four ponds could hold fish at times but may freeze solid during some years.

55 Unnamed Ponds (Lime Springs)

These ponds on the park side of the lower North Fork of the Flathead between Glacier Rim and Blankenship likely contain a few smaller cutthroat but may make an adventurous day of exploring.

Waterton River Drainage

56 Waterton River

Location: 12 02 88 305 E 54 26 697 N

Length: 12.4 miles

Species: EBT/C, LWFR, LT/R, RT/R

For much of its journey from Nahsukin Lake to Waterton Lake, the Waterton River is full of brook trout, especially in the area of Kootenai Lakes. Near Kootenai Lakes, the river bottom is swampy, and fishing from shore is often not an option. Very little of the river is accessible by trail, and only certain sections receive any angling pressure. The easiest way to fish it is to stay at Waterton River Backcountry Campground near Waterton Lake or to visit Kootenai Lakes Backcountry Campground. The brook trout in the river often take lures but can be a little fussy about rising in still water. It is best to wait until after spring runoff to fish the river, which then is more like a creek. Your best bet is to try some yellow-and-black Panther Martins or look for a faster riffle and place a stimulator with a dropper nymph such as a pheasant tail. Fishing with a yellow Marabou muddler or olive woolly bugger in early morning can take bigger fish.

Use is light, except at the outlet of Kootenai Lakes, which gets fished almost every day in the summer. The upper stretches of the river are inaccessible by trail and offer unfished waters for the bushwhacking angler. Be careful not to get sucked into the muddy areas above the lakes. The closest access to the Waterton River is less than a mile from Goat Haunt Ranger Station. To access the ranger station, take the ferry from Waterton in Alberta. From the station, hike 0.7 mile to Rainbow Falls along the river, or turn west across the bridge toward the Boulder Pass Trail and fish the river down to the inlet on Waterton Lake. You can also hike 2.8 miles (flat and easy) to Kootenai Lakes and fish up past the lakes (difficult and mucky) or downstream to where Camp Creek enters the river, which is one of the better spots for fly-fishing.

57 Waterton Lakes

Location: 12 02 88 413 E 54 26 612 N

Elevation: 4,196 ft

Area: 992 acres

Species: LT/C, LWF/C, EBT/C, RT/R, NP/R

Fishing the Waterton Lakes area of Glacier National Park is entirely dependent upon access from Waterton Lakes National Park. Waterton provides all the amenities of a tourist destination and offers good visitor information. It

Waterton River Drainage

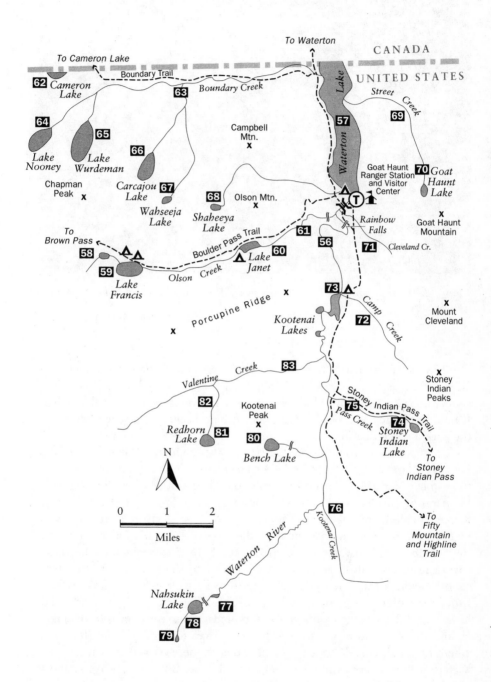

One of the most picturesque border crossings in the world, Wateron Lake. MICHAEL SAMPLE PHOTO

also has a boat launch. While you are in Waterton in Canada, you may consider fishing several lakes in Waterton Lakes National Park, including Cameron Lake and Lower Waterton Lake. However, remember that when fishing in Canada you need a Canadian fishing license, and when fishing in the park a special permit, available at the visitor center, is required.

The main access route to the Waterton Lakes country in Glacier National Park is by boat across Waterton Lake. The boat runs at regular intervals and the trip is reasonably priced. It allows you to access otherwise very inaccessible parts of Glacier National Park, including Lake Francis and Lake Janet, Kootenai Lakes, and the upper Waterton River. One of my favorite rides is to take the *International* across the lake, day hike to Kootenai Lakes, and take the boat back. This water route crosses the border, so remember that bear spray can be difficult to get across the border into Canada, and you are better off buying a can when you get there (if available). Waterton Lake is best fished by trolling in a motorized boat. The lake area is often windy and always cold. Large lake trout, up to 30 pounds, cruise the depths of the lake, eating whitefish and brook trout. The best places for fishing from shore are where Boundary Creek comes into the lake on the west side and where the Waterton River empties into the head of the lake. Both waterways support brook trout. Fly-fishing for whitefish can provide other angler entertainment.

Waterton Lake can produce some trophy-sized lake trout for anglers with a boat. I suggest some heavy metal lures and bait rigs with cowbells trolled at about 100 feet deep, except near the inlets, where you will have to troll in shallower water. If you are casting from shore at either inlet or any place along shore, be sure to use larger lures and let them sink before retrieving them.

58 Unnamed Lake (Thunderbird Pond)

59 Lake Francis

Location: 12 02 80 707 E 54 24 780 N

Elevation: 5,255 ft

Area: 87 acres

Species: RT/C

The cool cascades from the snowfield of Dixon Glacier provide Lake Francis with a deep blue color and a spectacular backdrop for fishing. The lake supports a large population of rainbows, some up to 4 pounds. They are often finicky but when rising can provide lots of action. Water from Thunderbird Glacier also pours into the lake from Olson Creek, right near the Lake Fran-

Calm waters of Lake Francis.

cis Backcountry Campground. This is the most popular place at the lake to fish and a good place for lure-fishing. If the fish are not rising to flies, try lure-fishing or nymphing in the inlet. Consider bringing your sinking line and fish a woolly worm or bitch creek nymph stripped slowly across the bottom.

Lake Francis is a hard campsite to get a permit for, and there are only two sites at the Lake Francis Backcountry Campground, which is a popular destination for people hiking over Boulder and Brown Passes. Anglers have to compete with lots of non-anglers for sites. It is 6.5 miles from the Goat Haunt Ranger Station to Lake Francis on the Boulder Pass Trail, which does not go directly to the lake. You have to take a 0.2-mile spur trail to the south off the Boulder Pass Trail.

60 Lake Janet

Location: 12 02 84 863 E 54 25 150 N

Elevation: 4,810 ft

Area: 34 acres

Species: RT/R

Lake Janet is not a place to spend a lot of time fishing. Occasionally a couple of trout rise on the placid surface of the lake, but they probably came downstream from Lake Francis and will most likely go back to Francis for the winter. Lake Janet is shallow, clear, and probably freezes solid in the winter. It is possible to catch fish here, and you may chase a rising fish around the lake, but do not expect a lot of action and be prepared to get skunked. Try Francis instead. Do not fish unless you see rising fish, and then use very light leader and small patterns.

There is light to zero angler use but moderate hiker use of the two sites at the Lake Janet Backcountry Campground. From Goat Haunt Ranger Station, follow Boulder Pass Trail south for 3.5 miles, with a slight climb, to Lake Janet.

61 Olson Creek

Location: 12 02 87 654 E 54 26 143 N

Length: 4.3 miles

Species: RT/R

Olson Creek joins the Waterton River right below the suspension bridge on the Boulder Pass Trail. It doesn't hold many fish, and you are better off fishing one of the lakes or in the Waterton River.

62 Cameron Lake

Location:

Elevation: 5,445 ft

Area: 35 acres

Species: RT/C, EBT/C, WCT/C

Accessible by a short drive from Waterton Townsite in Waterton Lakes National Park, this lake is partially in Glacier National Park. It is a popular destination of Canadian anglers and a nice visit while in Waterton.

63 Boundary Creek

Location: 12 02 87 630 E 54 30 889 N

Length: 5.9 miles

Species: EBT/C

Boundary Creek may be your best bet for creek fishing in the Waterton area. It's reasonably accessible by hiking around Waterton Lake or, more appropriately, taking the shuttle to Goat Haunt and fishing it on the hike back to Waterton Townsite.

64 Lake Nooney

65 Lake Wurdeman

66 Carcajou Lake

67 Wahseeja Lake

68 Shaheeya Lake

69 Street Creek

70 Goat Haunt Lake

71 Cleveland Creek

Location: 12 02 88 078 E 54 26 441 N

Length: N/A

Species: EBT/R

This small Goat Haunt area creek doesn't hold fish most of the year and runs pretty low in late summer.

72 Camp Creek

Location: 12 02 87 590 E 54 23 236 N

Length: N/A

Species: EBT/R

Camp Creek enters the Waterton River just below Kootenai Lakes. That spot gets fished plenty, but the rest of the creek sees little action.

73 Kootenai Lakes

Location: 12 02 287 E 54 23 133 N

Elevation: 4,400 ft

Area: 57 acres

Species: EBT/C, RT/R

Kootenai Lakes is a popular day-hike destination of many people who ride the ferry across Waterton Lake. More noted for its moose population than for its fishing, the lake does, however, offer good fishing for large brook trout, up to 3 pounds. Most people arrive at the foot of the lowest lake, right near the Kootenai Lakes Backcountry Campground, and throw in a lure. This area is the most fished—and the least likely place to catch fish. You will have better luck if you bring a float tube or neoprene waders that you do not mind getting muddy and work your way to the upper lakes, which offer much better fishing, basically because they are hard to reach. The thick willows and churned-up, muddy bottom are good for moose but not so good for getting around the lakes.

Fly-fishing can be good when the moose are not stirring up the waters. Try light green or yellow caddis imitations and damsel fly nymphs. If the lakes are muddy, try some packed-in worms or bait. Woolly buggers and leeches are also effective flies for the murky waters. The lakes are best fished after high water. Hike 2.8 flat miles from Goat Haunt Ranger Station after taking the boat across Waterton Lake from Waterton Townsite. The upper lakes and the opposite shore of the lower lake receive little fishing pressure.

Kootenai Lakes.

74 Stoney Indian Lake

Location: 12 02 89 786 E 54 18 695 N

Elevation: 6,325 ft

Area: 10 acres

Species: WCT/R

Stoney Indian Lake has one of the cooler names in the park (named for the Stoney branch of the Assiniboines) and it is one of the most desired campsites in the park. In fact, I can't remember the last time I talked with someone who both fished and obtained a permit at Stoney Indian Lake. Hiking by the lake, I've seen the occasional rise and heard secondhand of people catching fish there. From the looks of it, wet line and bead-head nymphs or woolly worms may be in order. Access Stoney Indian Lake first by getting lucky and getting a permit for it and then by hiking up from Goat Haunt (very steep and not the preferred route) or making an extended trip through the Belly to Goat Haunt.

75 Pass Creek

Location: 12 02 86 916 E 54 19 835 N

Length: N/A

Species: EBT/R

Those privileged enough to stay at the Pass Creek Patrol Cabin here are likely the only people that ever fish the lower reaches of this creek, which should hold a few brookies.

76 Kootenai Creek

Location: 12 02 86 362 E 54 16 503 N
Length: N/A
Species: EBT/R

77 Unnamed Lake (Lower Nahsukin)

Location: 12 02 82 453 E 54 13 319 N
Elevation: 5,100 ft
Area: N/A
Species: EBT/R

This lake is a small lake visible from the trail up Fifty Mountain from the Waterton Valley. There appear to be no barriers to prevent the Waterton River brook trout population from exploiting this remote habitat. However, it would be a hard bushwhack from anywhere to find out.

78 Nahsukin Lake

79 Unnamed Lake (Upper Nahsukin)

80 Bench Lake

81 Redhorn Lake

82 South Fork of Valentine Creek

Location: 12 02 82 885 E 54 20 459 N
Length: 6.9 miles
Species: EBT/C

83 Valentine Creek

Location: 12 02 86 878 E 54 21 125 N

Length: 2.7 miles

Species: EBT/C

There is no reason to believe the fishing is not as good here as it is at Kootenai Lakes and in the Waterton River. The creek is hard to get to, however. The best way to get there is to make a base camp at the Kootenai Lakes Backcountry Campground and bushwhack from the Waterton River Trail, a couple of miles south of the campground. Ernest J. Kinnie wrote about Valentine Creek in his *Fishing Guide to Glacier National Park*, published in 1960: "Some time ago this creek was considered to have the best cutthroat trout fishing in the Park. Due to the drop in number of hikers during the Second World War, and the subsequent disuse of the Valentine Creek Trail, few people fish Valentine Creek now. There is no particular reason to believe that the quality of fishing has changed." One thing that probably has changed is the species of fish: brook trout now dominate the drainage. Spinners, leech flies, woolly buggers, and many attractor patterns should catch fish.

Valentine Creek may not seem so remote when looking at the map, but other factors make it an impractical day or overnight trip. The creek is best fished in late August or September, when the muck is shallower than during the rest of the season. Access Valentine Creek from Goat Haunt Ranger Station on Waterton Lake or stay at Kootenai Lakes and day hike or (more appropriately) day bushwhack. From Goat Haunt Ranger Station, hike 2.8 miles on the Waterton River Trail to the backcountry campground at Kootenai Lakes and make a base camp for several days. Then hike about 1.5 miles toward Fifty Mountain and cut across the bog of the Waterton River near the old Porcupine Lookout Trail. Be careful not to get lost or drown in the muck.

Belly River Drainage

84 Belly River

Location: 12 03 03 840 E 54 30 403 N (Border)

Length: 13.6 miles

Species: BT/C, RT/R, AG/R, MWF/R, BT/R

The Belly River is one of the few places in Montana where you might catch brook, rainbow, bull, and lake trout and arctic grayling in the same river. The Belly River is not an exceptionally productive fishery, but it is connected to several productive lakes, which yield trophy-sized grayling and lake trout. For a day trip, the only way to fish the Belly River is to hike down to it and fish up the stream for a couple of hours, then hike out. To fish nearly all the lakes in the Belly River region, you have to backpack in or take a horse. To do either, you need a backcountry permit. The Belly is a meandering river, fed by Old Sun Glacier. In the spring, the river suffers from high muddy water. In the fall, it looks more like a small stream.

The Belly does receive a fair number of visitors, but most are concentrated along the sections right next to the Belly River Trail and around the campsites at the Gable Creek Backcountry Campground near the Belly River Ranger

The Belly River.

Belly River Drainage

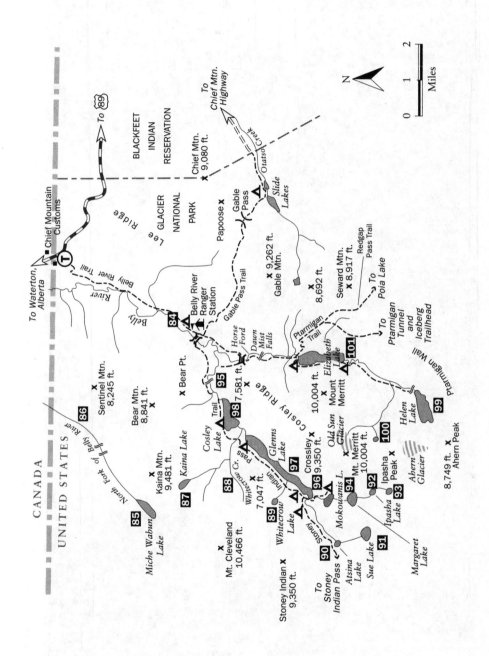

Dawn Mist Falls on the Belly River.

Station. The fish are finicky and often hard to catch during the day, but in the evening you can usually get an 8-inch brookie or two without much effort. From fertile Elizabeth Lake, the grayling and rainbow populations sometimes drift downstream, making it possible to catch bigger fish in the river. Also, because there are lake trout in Glenn and Cosley Lakes, it is possible to catch large predatory fish in the river.

From the Belly River Ranger Station to the Canadian border, the river is flat, skirted by dry meadows, and meanders toward the Canadian Plain. It suffers from spring scouring, but as the water drops and clears it has a productive population of ants and hoppers along the banks, and some of the bigger runs hold healthy populations of aquatic insects. When it is slow during the day, I often recommend trying a nymph imitation and fishing the tails of the holes. As evening approaches go back to a small parachute Adams or grizzly Wulff. The brookies, especially, feed on the surface before sundown. There are bigger rainbows in this stretch, so do not be surprised if you get one over 16 inches long. The upper section, from Elizabeth Lake to the Belly River Ranger Station, has more rapids and fewer meanders but still holds fish. It is tough bushwhacking up from the backcountry campground at Gable Creek, but access is easier at the horse ford before Dawn Mist Falls. This stretch above the ford holds large grayling and small-to-large rainbows, but the water is clear and the fish spook easily, so walk stealthily. It is fairly easy to pull small rainbows out of the run-out below but treacherous to fish right at the base of the falls. Above the falls, the river is mostly rapids and holds few fish, except for several side pools and the extended outlet of Elizabeth Lake. It is hard to fish with a spoon in this small river, so I recommend flies or packed-in bait. For flies, I recommend bitch creek nymph, Montana nymph, parachute Adams, bucktail caddis, or grizzly Wulff. During the day, action on top is slow and I recommend trying a nymph fished deep and slow. Also try terrestrial imitations such as foam beetles or black irresistibles. Mornings and evenings, the mayfly hatches bring the smaller fish to the surface.

If you do choose a spoon, I recommend a small Cyclone fished through the deep part of the holes. Cast just where the water cascades off the rocks into the pool. The water will sweep the lure into deeper water, like a small fry swept into the hole. Remember to cut off at least one treble hook to allow for releasing fish without killing them. Worms almost always work if you plan to keep fish.

Heaviest use concentrates around the Belly River Ranger Station and the Gable Creek Backcountry Campground, but it would not be considered heavy by most anglers. Because there are better destinations beyond, most of the traffic is through-hikers destined for Stoney Indian Pass and anglers headed for Elizabeth Lake. From Chief Mountain Customs, the Belly River is accessible by a well-worn, three-lane hiker and horse trail. You cannot see the river until about 3 miles down, but as soon as you stop descending you can walk to the west to fish. There is also a faint route on the west side of the river, across the suspension bridge on the Stoney Indian Pass Trail, less than 0.5 mile west of the Belly River Ranger Station. You can follow this faint path north down the river until you spot a rising fish.

85 Miche Wabun Lake

86 North Fork of the Belly River

Location: 12 02 98 505 E 54 30 629 N

Length: 4.5 miles

Species: BT/C, RT/R, EBT/R

Closed to fishing to facilitate the recovery of bull trout. Check current regulations.

87 Kaina Lake

88 Whitecrow Creek

Location: 12 02 97 101 E 54 21 673 N

Length: 3.5 miles

Species: RT/R, MWF/R

This tributary to the Mokowanis River may contain a few fish but is raging in the spring and a small sterile stream in the fall. It may be affected by area closures between Glenns and Cosley Lakes. *Check current regulations.*

89 Whitecrow Lake

90 Atsina Lake

91 Sue Lake

92 Ipasha Lake

93 Unnamed Lake (Above Ipasha Lake)

94 Margaret Lake

95 Mokowanis River

Location: 12 03 00 783 E 54 22 595 N

Length: 4.2 miles

Species: RBT/R, EBT/R, MWF/R, LT/R

Mokowanis River has the interesting distinction of being the longest river that starts and ends entirely within Glacier National Park (McDonald Creek would be, but it is a creek). Above Glenns Lake it doesn't hold much in the way of fish, and historically the section between Glenns and Cosley has been closed to fishing. *Check current regulations.* However, that section doesn't hold many fish, either. For the most part you are better off fishing in Mokowanis, Glenns, and Cosley Lakes than in the Mokowanis River. Many hikers stop and fish the large pool below Gros Ventre Falls, but often if you miss the first couple of strikes you'll get skunked. In addition, when the Mokowanis River is still raging the current is too strong to fish.

Gros Ventre Falls on the Mokowanis River.

96 Mokowanis Lake

Location: 12 02 93 649 E 54 17 733 N

Elevation: 4,981 ft

Area: 35 acres

Species: EBT/C

Fishing here can be slow, but Monty Parratt spreads rumors of mammoth brook trout in the old days. He recommends fishing the marshy areas with strong-scented flies, lures, or bait. You can probably count on a few 8- to 10-inch brookies, if you can tie on your fly without severe mosquito bites. Action can be slow on the surface and packed-in worms may be the way to go. Also try the stream above and below the lake.

The lake sees very light hiker use and even lighter angler use. There are only two campsites and an insane mosquito population, which you cannot smoke out because no fires are allowed here. Just past the end of Glenns Lake, turn south (left) for Mokowanis Lake, which is an easy 1.3-mile walk.

97 Glenns Lake

Location: 12 02 96 696 E 54 21 462 N

Elevation: 4,862 ft

Area: 266 acres

Species: LT/A, MWF/C, RT/R

Glenns Lake has a healthy but rarely fished population of lake trout, with generally spotty fishing, but the outlet makes for decent dry-fly water for a few rainbows and whitefish. Lures and worms take some fish in the shallower water of Glenns Lake. A small parachute Adams or a bead-head hare's ear nymph is a good fly for the evening hatch at the outlet. During the day I suggest using lures.

Neither inlet proves good for fly-fishing, and only the deeper parts of the head of the lake harbor lake trout. Sitting on the bridge below White Quiver Falls, the water may look pretty and be some of the cleanest on this planet, but the shallows near the inlets don't seem to hold fish.

Glenns Lake gets many hiker visitors because of four nearby campgrounds, but the lake is not known for its fishing. There are four sites at the foot of Glenns and three at the head, plus five at Mokowanis Junction and two at Mokowanis Lake. The lake is best fished in late September when the lake trout are in shallow water. Access the lake from Chief Mountain Customs by hiking along the Belly River Trail 6.1 miles to the ranger station, then turning right (west) onto the Stoney Indian Pass Trail, crossing the Belly River. You will pass Cosley Lake and, after a total of 10.2 miles, reach the foot of Glenns Lake, where there is a nice, grassy campground. The trail is well worn and well marked.

The campground at the head of Glenns Lake offers most visitors a night of rest prior to climbing Stoney Indian Pass, but those in search of large lake trout may want to stay a couple of days.

98 Cosley Lake

Location: 12 02 98 956 E 54 22 782 N

Elevation: 4,842 ft

Area: 231 acres

Species: LT/C, RT/R, MWF/R

Cosley Lake has some very large lake and rainbow trout, but they are not easy to catch. Traditionally, fishing for lake trout involves trolling with a big spoon, but you will never see a boat on this lake; even if you could carry one in, no motors are allowed. I still suggest a large silver spoon fished as deep as you can get it. The lake trout move into the shore a little in the evening, so you might want to nap in the afternoon and fish later. Cosley Campground has a nice gravelly beach perfect for worm-fishing off the bottom for big lake trout.

If you must fly-fish, hike west up the lake until the trail passes by the end of the lake. Here you can wade and fish for cruising rainbows, but be careful of the many downed logs. Fly-fishing is not recommended for lake trout. The lake is best fished in the fall near the inlet and when the lake trout come in close to shore.

There is a campground with four sites about 0.7 mile up the lake on the north side. It receives heavy hiker use for routes over Stoney Indian Pass (one of the most desired overland routes in the park), but light fishing pressure. The trail from Chief Mountain Customs is well worn. It is 8.7 miles to the Cosley Backcountry Campground. You can stay at the foot of Glenns Lake instead, which offers fishing at both Cosley and Glenns Lakes and easy access to the dry-fly area near the head of Cosley, if it is not closed for eagle nesting.

99 Helen Lake

100 Unnamed Lake (Below Old Sun Glacier)

101 Elizabeth Lake

Location: 12 03 00 341 E 54 18 721 N

Elevation: 4,892 ft

Area: 194 acres

Species: AG/C, RT/C

Fly-fishing Elizabeth Lake in a sheltered cove.

Elizabeth Lake is well known as a good lake for fishing. The primary reason for this is the big (up to 3 pounds), hungry arctic grayling. The view is spectacular and it is a big lake, so you can always find a quiet place to fish. The most unique thing about Elizabeth Lake is the evening mayfly hatch. Big, gray mayflies come off the surface in considerable numbers and a feeding frenzy ensues. The grayling feed vigorously on top, and the generally smaller rainbows follow suit.

I recommend a #12 gray Wulff for the evening, but your favorite mayfly attractor pattern will usually catch fish. Lures with silver and red work well, especially fished from the inlet or one of the coves along the west side of the lake.

Hikers use the backcountry campground at the foot of Elizabeth Lake heavily, with most of the campers making a day trip to Helen Lake. The backcountry campground at the head of Elizabeth Lake has less of a view but is not on the way to anyplace, so it receives less fishing and hiking pressure. Access the lake by hiking 9.3 miles from Chief Mountain Customs or 9.8 miles from the Iceberg Lake Trailhead northwest of Swiftcurrent Lodge (a much more difficult hike). Either way it is an overnight trip and requires a backcountry use permit for an overnight stay.

McDonald Creek Drainage

102 McDonald Creek

Location: 11 07 21 219 E 53 76 724 N

Length: 25.8 miles

Species: WCT/C, MWF/R, RT/R, EBT/R, BT/R, LT/R

McDonald Creek should really be called McDonald River, and it probably would be in many parts of the country. McDonald Creek is the longest creek starting and ending in the park.

In the early 1980s, McDonald Creek was a sight akin to Alaskan rivers during the salmon run. A successful Kokanee stocking program in Flathead Lake produced fall spawning runs of tens of thousands of salmon packed in so thick you could almost walk across the creek on their backs. Eagles would flock here, crowding the tree branches, and a few grizzlies would come down to the river to feed on the high-protein fish meal. This population of Kokanee collapsed, mostly due to the predation of another non-native species—lake trout—and the introduction of a mysis shrimp *(Mysis relicta)* into Flathead Lake.

Upper McDonald Creek can be fun fishing for small cutthroats.

McDonald Creek Drainage

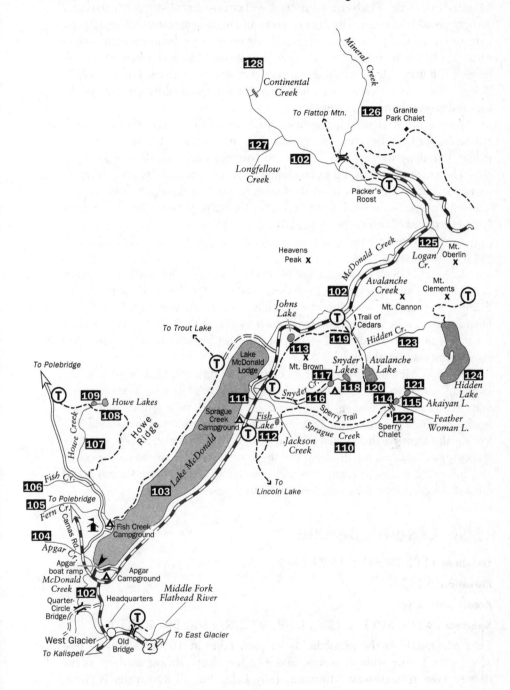

128 Continental Creek

Mineral Creek

126 To Flattop Mtn. Granite Park Chalet

127 Longfellow Creek

102

Packer's Roost

Heavens Peak **X**

McDonald Creek

125 Logan Cr.

Mt. Oberlin **X**

102 Avalanche Creek **X** Mt. Clements **X**

Mt. Cannon

Trail of Cedars

Johns Lake

Hidden Cr. **123**

To Trout Lake

Lake McDonald Lodge

113 X Mt. Brown

119

Snyder Lakes

Avalanche Lake

124 Hidden Lake

To Polebridge

109 Howe Lakes

108

Howe Ridge

117

Snyder Cr.

118

120

121

115 Akaiyan L.

107

111

116

Sperry Trail

114

122 Feather Woman L.

Sperry Chalet

Sprague Creek Campground

Fish Lake

112

Jackson Creek

Sprague Creek

110

106 Fish Cr.

103

To Lincoln Lake

105 To Polebridge

Fern Cr.

104 Apgar Cr.

Camas Rd.

Fish Creek Campground

Apgar boat ramp

McDonald Creek

Apgar Campground

Middle Fork Flathead River

102 Headquarters

Quarter-Circle Bridge

West Glacier

To Kalispell

Old Bridge

2

To East Glacier

As for the fishing in McDonald Creek between Lake McDonald and the Middle Fork of the Flathead, your creel will consist of mostly cutthroats and an occasional lake trout. The area receives an amazing amount of fishing pressure and historically has been catch-and-release with artificial flies and single-hook lures only, such as a Johnson weedless spoon. The area offers very challenging still water, dry-fly fishing, especially upstream from the Quarter-Circle Bridge. The water is very clear, and fish are easily spooked by the drag of the line and larger diameter tippets.

Above Lake McDonald, the creek holds few fish, except above Packer's Roost. Upper stretches can offer good fishing for small- to medium-sized cutthroat, but many stretches are barren and you may have to walk a bit between fish. The creek is best fished in late summer when the water is low. Access it by parking at Packer's Roost off the Going-to-the-Sun Road and bushwhacking to the creek. Some sections right next to Going-to-the-Sun Road above the lake receive heavy fishing pressure, but most anglers are unsuccessful. On the upper sections, fishing right next to the road may feel like a cool thing to do, but it is not advised.

McDonald Creek between Lake McDonald and the Quarter-Circle Bridge is catch-and-release only. For fly-fishing, use smaller flies and finer tippets. Focus on presentation. For spin-fishing, use lures with gold and red. Downstream casts with erratic retrieves may take fish. Fishing may be slow for both lures and flies, but there is potential for big lake trout on lures and larger rainbows on the fly.

To access McDonald Creek at its confluence with the Middle Fork of the Flathead, drive to the Quarter-Circle Bridge. Just after the West Entrance Station and heading east on Going-to-the-Sun Road, turn left at the Glacier Institute sign. Stay right at the first intersection and turn left at the second, following the signs to the Quarter-Circle Bridge. You can also access the river from Apgar, walking north along the shore of Lake McDonald to the outlet and following it downstream. There is also good water where Camas Road crosses the creek just north of the turnoff to Apgar.

103 Lake McDonald

Location: 12 02 78 943 E 53 79 294 N

Elevation: 3,153 ft

Area: 7,048 acres

Species: LWF/A, MWF/A, LT/C, BT/R, WCT/R, KS/R, EBT/R, RT/R

Lake McDonald is the granddaddy of park lakes at 10 miles long, 7,048 acres, over a mile wide in places, and 472 feet deep, almost as deep as the deepest lake in northwest Montana, Tally Lake. But all that water is clean, nutrient-poor water from Upper McDonald Creek and doesn't support dense populations of fish.

In short, fishing Lake McDonald should involve a boat and a trolling rig. Fly-fishing from a boat at the inlet can be effective, but generally the lake trout do not take flies, and the cutthroat population is anorexic. Trolling with large silver spoons and cowbells or jigging for lake trout are successful ways to fish. Monty Parratt recommends fishing in late May to mid-June when the lake trout come out of the deep water to feed. There is light fishing pressure because most people do not bring their own boat; if they do, they generally just cruise or water-ski. The fishing from shore is not that good, so not many people do it. You can easily reach the lake at all the campgrounds and visitor facilities around it. There is a public boat ramp at Apgar and shore access at Fish Creek, Sprague Creek, and Apgar Campgrounds; Lake McDonald Lodge; and the bridge on the North Lake McDonald Lodge Road.

If you want to get serious, rent a boat or launch your own at the public boat ramp at Apgar. The lake is best fished in April or October.

104 Apgar Creek

Location: 12 02 78 862 E 53 79 079 N

Length: N/A

Species: WCT/R

Apgar Creek runs under the road just before the Fish Creek turnoff on the Camas Road heading north from Apgar. It should hold a few small cutthroat.

105 Fern Creek

Location: 12 02 79 662 E 53 81 805 N

Length: N/A

Species: WCT/R

Closed to fishing. Check current regulations.

106 Fish Creek

Location: 12 02 79 973 E 53 81 069 N

Length: N/A

Species: WCT/C

Closed to fishing, Check current regulations.

107 Howe Creek

Location: 12 02 78 787 E 43 83 655 N
Length: N/A
Species: WCT/R
Check current regulations.

108 Upper Howe Lake

Location: 12 02 79 594 E 53 87 656 N
Elevation: 4,106 ft
Area: 20 acres
Species: WCT/C, RS/C

Howe Lakes is a relatively gentle uphill day hike to a marshy peat bog with two lakes. Both lakes contain 6- to 8-inch westslope cutthroat, and the location offers a pleasant day trip without a lot of hiking. Be especially careful of nesting loons and other waterfowl in early summer. The biggest problem with fishing the lake is the shoreline. Walking on it feels like floating on a carpet, and much of it is floating islands of moss and grass. Be very careful when wading around the lake not to step off an island and go for a swim. You will

The author with a Howe Lake cutthroat. Denny Gignoux photo

get your feet wet fishing this lake, and only waders can prevent that. Move around the lake to spots where the shore islands drop off suddenly; cast a woolly worm or a green damsel fly nymph quietly on the calm water. Strip in your wet fly and feel for a strike. Muddlers and leech flies should do well because redside shiners also inhabit the lakes. You might also try a parachute Adams, which once brought in several fish for me. The action is fast at each spot you fish but cools off quickly after you have caught your first fish, often on your first soft cast. Move to the next spot and try again.

The lake receives moderate use, because of the short hike, but mostly just by hikers. There is no campground and no overnight use. Drive 5.4 miles north on the Inside North Fork Road from Fish Creek Campground on the northwest corner of Lake McDonald. The Howe Lakes Trailhead is on the right (east) side of the road.

109 Lower Howe Lake

Location: 12 02 79 070 E 53 87 646 N

Elevation: 4,106 ft

Length: 8 acres

Species: WCT/C, RS/C

The first lake you see heading to Howe Lakes is the smaller lower lake. Have no fear; the bigger lake and more shoreline are near (see number 108).

110 Sprague Creek

Location: 12 02 87 469 E

Length: N/A

Species: EBT/R

Sprague Creek has never been known for fishing, and you are probably better off fishing in Lake McDonald for lake trout, Fish Lake for cutthroat, or Snyder Creek if you want to catch a few brookies.

111 Jackson Creek

Location: 12 02 87 636 E 53 88 132 N

Length: N/A

Species: EBT/R

This small creek enters Lake McDonald between Sprague Creek and the first turnoff to Lake McDonald Lodge.

Fish Lake.

112 Fish Lake

Location: 12 02 89 249 E 53 86 908 N

Elevation: 4,148 ft

Area: 8 acres

Species: WCT-YCT Hybrid/R

Fish Lake is shallow and swampy looking but does support a sparse population of small cutthroats. The lake is more like a pond and is not a scenic destination for most park visitors. An Adams irresistible should be sufficient for catching these little cutthroats, but do not be overconfident, do not splash into the lake, and do not slap the water. A little stealth or a worm may be necessary. The lake gets fairly light use. It is not at the top of anybody's vacation destination list, but because of its close proximity to Lake McDonald Lodge, it does get some day-hiker traffic. Access it from Lake McDonald Lodge via the Sperry Trail; go west (right) onto the Snyder Ridge Trail, 2.4 miles from the trailhead.

113 Johns Lake

114 Feather Woman Lake

115 Akaiyan Lake

116 Snyder Creek

Location: 12 02 87 792 E 53 88 693 N

Length: N/A

Species: EBT/C, WCT/R

Snyder Creek is not an obvious place to fish, and most of the fishing in it happens right off Going-to-the-Sun Road. You have to bushwhack off the Sperry Trail from the footbridge upstream or downstream to fish for small brookies and cutthroats. The fish are small and the stream is overgrown, so shorter fly rods and lighter spin rigs are recommended. Try to get away from the road or the trail and fish the pocket water with an orange stimulator or yellow humpy. Spin-fishing is not possible in the shallow water of the creek, but worms can be very successful.

Hike 1.8 miles on the Sperry Trail from Lake McDonald Lodge. When the trail crosses the bridge over Snyder Creek, fish up or down. You can also fish up from Going-to-the-Sun Road, but this is less promising.

117 Lower Snyder Lake

Location: 12 02 93 647 E 53 89 482 N

Elevation: 5,210 ft

Area: 6 acres

Species: WCT/A

Snyder Lakes makes a good overnight fishing trip for a family with kids. The hike in is not that hard, and the fishing is really easy. The fish are small, but they will take almost any fly or lure. If you get bored catching fish in the lake, try the stream between the two lakes; the steep cascading pools hold fish. Watch the nettles above the lake. Almost anything—lures, flies, or worms—should catch fish.

The lake gets heavy day use for both fishing and hiking, but overnight pressure is light. There are only three sites at the Snyder Lakes Backcountry Campground. Hike 4.4 miles from Lake McDonald Lodge on a gradual uphill to lower Snyder Lake. A short trail follows the southeast shore of the lake around to a talus slope, which offers free casting and pleasant views.

118 Upper Snyder Lake

119 Avalanche Creek

Location: 12 02 92 788 E 53 95 519 N

Length: N/A

Species: WCT/R

Generally not considered a fishing destination. Take your family hiking here instead or fish Avalanche Lake. *Check current regulations.*

120 Avalanche Lake

Location: 12 02 94 838 E 53 93 230 N

Elevation: 3,905 ft

Area: 57 acres

Species: WCT/C

The fish here may be the key to the recovery of cutthroat trout west of the Continental Divide. The cascades in Avalanche Gorge have prevented inter-breeding with non-native fish and the remaining native population in Avalanche Lake may be used for future restocking efforts as a source of genet-ically pure westslope cutthroat trout. The fishing gets better as you get farther away from the inlet where the main trail reaches the area. The heavy fishing

Because of its beauty, Avalanche Lake draws a lot of anglers and hikers. MICHAEL SAMPLE PHOTO

pressure on the outlet side of the lake makes fishing from a float tube near the inlet the best way to fish, and Avalanche is not too far to haul one. The lake is visited often because it is a beautiful lake with good fishing and a pleasant hike. It is an easy but slightly uphill 2.9-mile hike from Avalanche Campground.

121 Unnamed Lake (Below Sperry Glacier)

122 Unnamed Lake (Sperry Campground Pond)

123 Hidden Creek

Location: 12 02 94 391 E 53 94 170 N

Length: N/A

Species: YCT/R

The only fishable sections of Hidden Creek are those near Hidden Lake; the rest of the creek is too steep to hold fish. *Check current regulations before fishing in the stream near the lake.*

124 Hidden Lake

Location: 12 02 97 292 E 53 95 795 N

Elevation: 6,375 ft

Area: 277 acres

Species: YCT/C

Hidden Lake is one of the highest lakes in the park that supports a sustainable population of fish. It was the first lake in the park to go catch-and-release because of heavy use and its location in prime bear habitat. It also has a large population of non-native Yellowstone cutthroat trout, up to 18 inches long. The cruising cutthroats often pick mayflies off a glassy surface, and catching them takes some patience. On windy days, try stripping in a yellow muddler on wet line. If you bring in a float tube, fish a shrimp pattern deep, stripped in slowly. The trail to Hidden Lake is probably the most popular day hike in the park. Most of the pressure concentrates at the outlet, because that is where the trail reaches the lake. The fishing pressure gradually decreases across the outlet and up the west shore.

Access Hidden Lake by hiking 3 miles from the visitor center at Logan Pass. The trail starts just behind the visitor center on a boardwalk. You may have trouble finding a parking spot at Logan Pass during peak season. *The outlet is periodically closed to fishing. Check current regulations.*

125 Logan Creek

Location: 12 02 96 798 E 54 00 327 N

Length: N/A

Species: WCT/R

This tributary of McDonald Creek harbors small cutthroats, but they can be few and far between.

126 Mineral Creek

Location: 12 02 92 405 E 54 03 578 N

Length: N/A

Species: WCT/C, MWF/R

Instead of trying to fish upper McDonald Creek, try hiking in toward Flattop Mountain from Packer's Roost. It is an easy hike. The stream is small and very clear. The cutthroat are sparse but not heavily fished. If you see one rising, you should be able to hook it. For flies, an Adams irresistible or pheasant tail nymph should do the trick. Worms are likely to work, but you will end up with several fish that are not big enough to eat. If you can cast a spinner in this shallow creek, my hat is off to you. Sparse fishing means there are usually no crowds here, but the easy access makes it a target for increased use in the future.

Access the creek by driving 23 miles east of West Glacier; look for an unmarked dirt access road on the left and turn onto it. (If you get to the first tunnel on Going-to-the-Sun Road, you have gone too far.) At the end of this short dirt road is the Packer's Roost Trailhead. From here, hike about 2 miles on the Flattop Mountain Trail to the suspension bridge over Mineral Creek. It is a short bushwhack, less than 0.5 mile, to McDonald Creek.

127 Longfellow Creek

Location: 12 02 88 416 E 54 06 485 N

Length: N/A

Species: WCT/C

This remote creek is better bear country than trout country. You may pick up a few small cutthroats, but an angler is better off fishing upper McDonald Creek.

128 Continental Creek

Location: 12 02 86 909 E 54 08 764 N

Length: N/A

Species: WCT/R

The very lowest portion of this remote creek may hold a few small cutthroats, but an angler is better off fishing upper McDonald Creek.

Saint Mary River Drainage

129 Saint Mary River

Location: 12 03 08 316 E 53 93 824 N

Length: 24 miles

Species: MWF/C, LWF/C, RT/C, LT/R, BT/R, WCT/R, NP/R

From Gunsight Lake to Saint Mary Falls, the river is slow and marshy. At times it holds an occasional rainbow or two, but access can be boggy, fishing can be slow, and the bugs can be tough. The Mirror Pond area of Upper Saint Mary River is willow-mosquito-moose heaven, boggy stillwater, with some riffles and holes. This section is best fished at low water and after a frost. Spin casters may out-fish fly casters on the still stretches. However, there are a few bigger rainbows for those willing to work for them. Luckily the hike is short and access is easy from Gunsight Overlook Trailhead.

The area between Saint Mary Falls and Saint Mary Lake holds large populations of whitefish, but the tricky current makes catching them difficult. It is better suited for baitfishing than for other types of fishing. However, the fly fisher with sinking line and a small bead-head nymph may take a few whitefish, too.

The river is pretty to fish and easily accessible near Going-to-the-Sun Road Bridge near Saint Mary Townsite. There you are best to fish dry flies. The deep pools and runs hold many rainbows and whitefish. For flies on the section below the lake, try hopper patterns or smaller mayfly patterns in the evening. In the early morning use fish streamers or woolly buggers. All day a pheasant tail nymph, fished properly by casting directly upstream on a riffle and letting it dead drift into a deeper channel or hole, should take fish. This section sees a lot of worms, so try something else for bait like a hopper or grub. Lure-fishing is difficult in the shallow stream, but if you go downstream toward the reservation you can pick up some big fish. In some waters you never know what you might catch, but here trout would be a start, then whitefish. You might even grab a pike that comes upstream from the lower backwaters to grab a meal of baby rainbows.

Drive into the east entrance after Saint Mary; heading west the first bridge you cross past the visitor center is over the Saint Mary River. To access the section above the lake, drive 0.3 mile past Baring Creek, heading west from Saint Mary on Going-to-the-Sun Road. (If you pass the Jackson Glacier Overlook you have gone too far.) Hike 1.2 miles to Saint Mary Falls and fish down to the lake. The inlet to the lake is boggy and very difficult bushwhacking, so reaching the inlet from the falls is no easy task. The river is heavily fished near the bridge at the outlet of Saint Mary Lake but receives less pressure above the lake.

130 Saint Mary Lake

Location: 12 03 20 114 E 54 02 151 N

Elevation: 4,484 ft

Area: 3896 acres

Species: LT/A, MWF/C, LWF/C, RT/R, BT/R, WCT

Saint Mary Lake is best fished by boat. You can catch fish from shore out of the lake, most likely on a spoon. As with most lakes, the inlet is a very good place to fish, but the inlet to Saint Mary Lake is a boggy bushwhack and uninviting to even the most veteran off-trail traveler. I would recommend taking your boat to the inlet, however.

You can fish the lake at the outlet, which is very accessible and receives heavy fishing pressure. I watched a guy change from flies to lures to flies and back to lures chasing the rising whitefish at the outlet. Finally, after three hours (that's how long he said he had been there), he brought in a lake trout on a little black-and-yellow Mepps. That lake trout was probably fishing for the little whitefish rising on the surface, but the guy was just so happy to catch a fish in Montana, the dream of many a visitor to our state.

Saint Mary Lake holds big fish, maybe the biggest in the park. On July 18, 1954, Mark Parratt caught a lake trout weighing forty-two pounds eight ounces that was 49 inches in length. The widest girth was 27 inches and the head was immense. When dressed the stomach revealed five fish, the largest a two-pound cutthroat trout, showing the known predatory nature of the lake

Mark Parratt with his 42-pound lake trout from the depths of Saint Mary Lake, 1954.

Saint Mary River Drainage

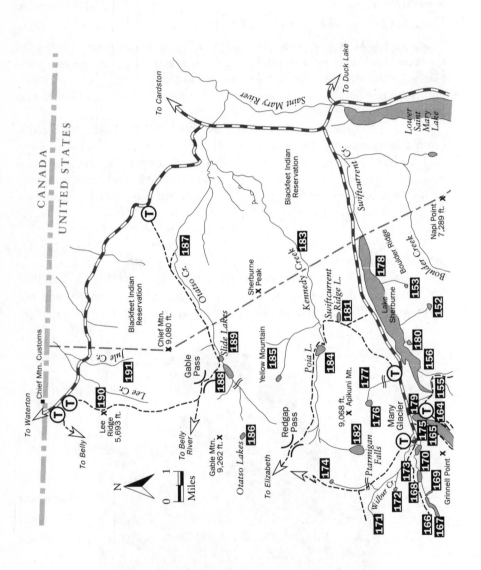

Saint Mary River Drainage

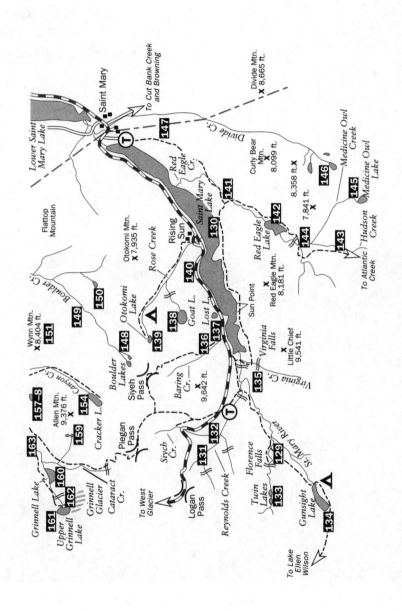

The outlet of Saint Mary Lake offers good evening fishing for whitefish and the lake trout that follow.

Saint Mary Lake from Otokomi Mountain.

trout. The other four fish included three good-sized mountain whitefish and a smaller rainbow trout. His fish gained honorable mention in the 1954 *Field and Stream* trophy list for lake trout.

You can fish anywhere along the north shore, which runs parallel to Going-to-the-Sun Road. You may have trouble getting down to the shore in spots where the bank is quite steep and eroded from the massive waves of wind coming off the Continental Divide. Any of these places could garner you fish, but action is slow and I suggest only casting to rising fish or fishing in the evening.

If you are adventurous, have a boat, or like bushwhacking, follow the south shore from the Red Eagle Lake Trailhead to the inlet of Red Eagle Creek. There should be a couple of big lake trout waiting for some poor little cutthroat to swim downstream from Red Eagle Lake. At the outlet, on a calm day whitefish will rise to well-drifted smaller dries. For the rest of the lake I recommend trolling a large silver spoon or casting assorted Mepps and Daredevles.

The only boat ramp on the lake is just west of Rising Sun and does not offer docking facilities. There is a turnoff and a trail down to the outlet of the lake 0.1 mile west of the Saint Mary River Bridge. A trail follows the lake from Sun Point to Saint Mary Falls. You can also turn south (left) 0.25 mile west of Saint Mary Townsite on Going-to-the-Sun Road. Drive 0.5 mile to the Red Eagle Lake Trailhead and follow the trail 0.25 mile to the shoreline. A short trail continues up the shore but peters out quickly. Use is heaviest at the foot of the lake; otherwise the lake receives little fishing pressure.

131 Reynolds Creek

The creek is fishless above the confluence of Saint Mary River due to Deadwood Falls and other cascades.

132 Siyeh Creek

133 Twin Lakes

134 Gunsight Lake

Location: 12 03 00517 E 53 89 198 N

Elevation: 5,300 ft

Area: 118 acres

Species: RT/C

There are two problems with fishing Gunsight Lake. First, it is almost always windy. Second, for half the summer the lake is too high from snowmelt to walk around the shore. Thick alders make shore navigation at high water almost impossible. Kim says it is pretty, though, and I agree. It is well worth the visit. If you cannot pull a 14- to 16-inch rainbow out of the lake, try the stream flowing out of it. The creek makes for fun, small-stream fishing for 6-inch rainbows. If you can make it to the inlet, I highly recommend it. Get away from the campground at the foot of the lake. Make your way around the north shore and work from the points. Use big, bushy dries on choppy water.

The campground has eight sites and the lake receives moderate day traffic from through-hikers making the 20-mile day hike to Lake McDonald. From Jackson Glacier Overlook, it is 6.2 miles of relatively flat hiking in the trees on Gunsight Pass Trail to Gunsight Lake. If you continue toward Gunsight Pass, there is a goat trail off the first switchback that can make it easier to get to the head of the lake.

135 Virginia Creek

Location: 12 03 07 760 E 53 93 607

Length: N/A

Species: MWF/R, RT/R

Saint Mary Lake is still a productive native fishery for lake trout. MONTY PARRATT
PHOTO

136 Baring Creek

Location: 12 03 09 206 E 53 94 407 N

Length: N/A

Species: WCT/R

137 Lost Lake

Location: 12 03 10 500 E 53 94 992 N

Elevation: 4,666 ft

Area: 2 acres

Species: EBT/C

The small, colorful brook trout in this lake see a lot of worms, flies, lures, and skinny-dippers, but it is still fairly common to catch a couple of 8-inch brookies on a small mayfly imitation or a worm. No native fish to worry about here. Access is across from an unmarked pullout just east of Sun Point.

138 Goat Lake

Goat Lake may not have any fish, but it looks impressive from Otokomi Mountain and at 69 acres is three times as big as Otokomi Lake.

139 Otokomi Lake

Location: 12 03 09 211 E 53 99 114 N

Elevation: 6,482 ft

Area: 22 acres

Species: YCT-RT Hybrids/C

Do not make the mistake of thinking you are going to start late, mosey on up to the lake, fish, and lazily stride back down. The hike is all uphill and harder than it looks on the map. Leave early and give yourself plenty of time. Hiking all day with a fishing rod does not count as fishing.

Otokomi contains healthy populations of hybrid Yellowstone cutthroats. The lake is deep and the water clear. The fishing slows significantly during the day, which is the only time to fish if you day hike. If you can get a permit, I highly recommend an overnight stay at the backcountry campground at Otokomi Lake.

Bring your wet line and fish a bead-head soft-hackle nymph or orange scud deep and slow. Try to get away from the outlet. You can cross Rose Creek and hike off-trail along the southern shore for a spot to fish. Fish dries only if you see rising fish during midday. In the evening, watch for rising trout

Otokomi Lake can be a cold one, dress appropriately. MARNIE SCHNEIDER PHOTO

on a mayfly hatch and tie on a gray Wulff. For bait, bring some worms and rig them just off the bottom. The lake is best fished after July because snow lingers until then. Use is moderate because of its proximity to Going-to-the-Sun Road, but few people get around the lake to fish. The Otokomi Lake Backcountry Campground just before the outlet has only three sites, accessed by hiking 5 miles uphill from the Rising Sun Camp Store.

140 Rose Creek

Location: 12 03 14 707 E 53 95 936 N

Length: 4.8 miles

Species: YCT-RT/R, WCT/R, MWF/R

Rose Creek, in it's lower reaches, slows to only a trickle and doesn't support much in the way of fish.

141 Red Eagle Creek

Location: 12 03 17 765 E 53 97 385 N

Length: 11.8 miles

Species: WCT-RT Hybrids/R, RT/R, BT/R, and MWF/R

Red Eagle Creek on the way to Red Eagle Lake.

Although the pools next to the trail look inviting, most of the creek is pretty sterile. The unstable gravel and loose conglomerate make the stream bank susceptible to spring flood scouring and anorexic insect populations. I recommend trying sections of the creek close to either Saint Mary Lake or Red Eagle Lake, where summer rainbows may move into the stream to feed.

Access Red Eagle Creek by turning south off Going-to-the-Sun Road, 0.25 mile west of Saint Mary Townsite. Drive 0.5 mile to the Red Eagle Trailhead. Then hike a little over 4 miles to the first suspension bridge over the creek. Fish upstream or downstream. You can also try the section above and below Red Eagle Lake from a base camp at the lake. You have to bushwhack almost 3 miles around Saint Mary Lake to get to the inlet of Red Eagle Creek, and when you get there you probably should fish in the inlet and not venture too far up the creek. There is light use due to generally spotty fishing and moderately difficult access.

142 Red Eagle Lake

Location: 12 03 15 745 E 53 92 147 N

Elevation: 4,722 ft

Area: 141 acres

Species: RT-YCT/C, RT/R, MWF/R, BT/R

In 1955 William D. Sands caught a sixteen-pound cutthroat trout in Red Eagle Lake for the state record that still stands. This of course is nothing compared to the thirty-three-pound world record rainbow trout that came out the chumming waters below Kootenai Dam, but it's still a little big for your average cutthroat. Back then they didn't have genetic experts on cutthroat, like Dr. Leo Marmell, who might have had the uninviting task of informing Mr. Sands that in fact his fish was a hybrid cutthroat and rainbow trout and disqualifying the state record. The state record for a cutt-bow hybrid is thirty pounds out of Ashley Lake. Imagine the possibilities.

No matter what you call them, they are big, and many anglers try to drag one out of the lake or the stream above and below it. Many fail, partially because so many are trying. One consequence of increased fishing is not damage to the fishery but smarter fish.

The most important advice I can give you is to camp at the lake and bring in a float tube. This is no easy task, but you need time to work the rising fish and to float a leech deep. Don't bank on fishing on the falls above or below the lake, because lots of other anglers fish those as well. You may end up watching a 20-inch trout deny fly after fly like it's seen them all.

During the day when the fish aren't rising and still in deep water, fish a wet line with a leech or woolly bugger deep. The fish have seen a lot of lures, but out in the middle of the lake and on the north shore they may be less wary and take a smaller red-and-gold Mepps or Daredevle. Worms may not work too well here, but you can give them a try. If you can gather grasshoppers outside the park and bring some in, fish them off the bottom in the falls above the lake or the drop below the lake.

Turn south (left) 0.25 mile west of Saint Mary Townsite on Going-to-the-Sun Road. Drive 0.5 mile to the Red Eagle Trailhead. Hike 7.7 miles to the foot of the lake. The trail is dry and relatively flat but takes at least two and one-half hours each way, so plan accordingly.

143 Hudson Creek

144 Medicine Owl Creek

145 Medicine Owl Lake

146 Unnamed Lake (Upper Divide Creek Lakes)

147 Divide Creek

Location: 12 03 20 927 E 54 02 383 N
Length: 9.2 miles

Species: BT/R, RT/R, MWF/R

Divide Creek looks very pretty from the Snow Goose during dinner, but you'd be hard pressed to drag very many fish out of it. It may hold some fish, but it's better left to the occasional spawner.

148 Boulder Lakes

Location: 12 03 07 769 E 54 00 374 N

Elevation: 6,402 ft

Area: N/A

Species: BT/R, RT/R, MWF/R

Closed to fishing. Check current regulations. I wish I'd gotten a chance to fish these lakes before they were closed to fishing in 2000, but they are still pretty to look at from Siyeh Pass, and the Boulder Valley provides excellent habitat for spawning fish from the Saint Mary River.

149 Boulder Creek

Location: 12 03 19 597 E 54 12 254 N

Length: 13.4 miles

Species: BT/R, RT/R, MWF/R

Closed to Fishing. Check current regulations.

150 Unnamed Lake (Below Flattop Ridge)

151 Unnamed Lake (Below Wynn Mountain)

152 Unnamed Lake (Boulder Ridge #1)

153 Unnamed Lake (Boulder Ridge #2)

154 Cracker Lake

Location: 12 03 06 004 E 54 02 507 N

Elevation: 5,910 ft

Area: 42 acres

Species: BT/C

Closed to fishing. Check current regulations. This lake contains a starving, stunted, and overpopulated stock of bull trout. At one time it was a popular place for beginners, but most anglers won't miss fishing Cracker Lake.

155 Allen Creek

Location: 12 03 06 214 E 54 07 109 N

Length: N/A

Species: BT/R

156 Canyon Creek

Location: 12 03 07 395 E 5407 965 N

Length: 4.2 miles

Species: EBT/R, BT/R

Check current regulations.

157 Falling Leaf Lake

158 Snow Moon Lake

159 Unnamed Lake (Allen Mountain Ponds)

160 Cataract Creek

Location: 12 03 04 440 E 54 07 205 N

Length: N/A

Species: EBT/C

The creek is best fished between Josephine and Swiftcurrent Lakes near what is sometimes called Stump Lake. This section holds a few good-sized brookies.

161 Upper Grinnell Lake

Thinking about carrying your fishing pole to Grinnell Glacier? Think again: no fish.

162 Grinnell Lake

Location: 12 03 01 650 E 54 05 050 N

Elevation: 5,080 ft

Area: 77 acres

Species: EBT/C

The lake offers slow fishing for brook trout because of the large amount of pale blue glacial flour from receding Grinnell Glacier. You can bushwhack your way to the inlet, but you might as well fish Josephine rather than make the effort. Float a woolly bugger deep. Brighter, flashier lures are better for this lake. The murky waters near the outlet and inlet offer good spots for a little bait-fishing. Bait-fishing tends to out-fish other methods in murky water.

From Many Glacier Hotel you can hike along the southern shore of Swiftcurrent Lake to either the North Shore Lake Josephine Trail or the South Shore Josephine Trail. Or you can take the boat across both lakes for the final 1-mile hike from the head of Lake Josephine to Grinnell Lake. There is heavy hiker use in the area, but you don't see a lot of people fishing.

163 Lake Josephine

Location: 12 03 03 946 E 54 06 418 N

Elevation: 4,920 ft

Area: 137 acres

Species: EBT/C, KS/R

The lake offers fair fishing for 10- to 12-inch brook trout. Because of the boat ride across Swiftcurrent and Josephine, you can reach the inlet without walking a mile from Many Glacier Hotel. Float a little Zug bug in the inlet or fish lures around the south side of the lake. A yellow rooster tail Mepps should do. You also might try the stream between Josephine and Swiftcurrent, which has some nice pools.

From Many Glacier Hotel you can hike along the southern shore of Swiftcurrent Lake to either the North Shore Lake Josephine Trail or the South Shore Josephine Trail. Just remember that you will see other people any time you hike in the Many Glacier Valley trail system.

164 Stump Lake (see Cataract Creek, number 160)

165 Swiftcurrent Creek

Location: 12 03 04 468 E 54 07 776 N

Length: 10.3 miles

Species: EBT/R

This sparsely populated creek doesn't support much of a fluvial population of trout; an angler is better off fishing the lakes connected to it.

166 Windmaker Lake

Location: 12 02 98 653 E 54 07 490 N

Elevation: 5,245 ft

Area: 19 acres

Species: EBT/C

The lake offers fast fishing for 8- to 10-inch brook trout and does not get fished that much. The shoreline is a little brushy, so casting a fly may not be too easy unless you bring a float tube. The short but difficult bushwhack from the Swiftcurrent Pass Trail keeps most people at Bullhead and Red Rock Lakes, so this is probably your best shot at having a lake to yourself, and a grizzly or two.

From the west end of the Swiftcurrent Motor Inn parking lot, hike about 4 miles toward Swiftcurrent Pass until you cross the creek from Windmaker Lake, then bushwhack to the lake. I don't recommend bushwhacking to Windmaker if you have never hiked off-trail in Glacier National Park before or if you are scared of bears. Use is light because of the lack of a trail.

167 Upper Bullhead Lake and

168 Lower Bullhead Lake

Location: 12 02 99 576 E 54 07 223 N

Elevation: 5,160 ft

Area: 38 acres

Species: EBT/C

These lakes offer fair fishing for 10- to 12-inch brook trout and get less pressure than Red Rock Lake. Fish the inlet of the upper lake from Windmaker Lake and work your way along the shore. Small Mepps and Krocodiles should work. I also would try to rig some worms off the bottom and take a nap along the shore. The Swiftcurrent Valley can be downright peaceful on a sunny day.

To access Bullhead Lakes, hike from the west end of the Swiftcurrent Motor Inn parking lot toward Swiftcurrent Pass until you see Bullhead Lakes 3.3 miles later. The hike is flat and friendly. There is heavy hiker use in the area, but only moderate fishing pressure concentrated near the trail.

169 Red Rock Lake

Location: 12 03 01 425 E 54 08 149 N

Elevation: 5,078 ft

Area: 36 acres

Species: EBT/C

The lake offers fair fishing for 10- to 12-inch brook trout but gets the most pressure of any of these lakes along Swiftcurrent Creek. The inlet is hard to fish because you have to wade out to an island to reach deep water. Dry-fly fishing in the lower falls is often productive during August when fish from the lake exploit stream hatches. The fish see a lot of worms and lures at the head of the lake, so try to get around to the east end, and you might even consider fishing the creek down to Fishercap Lake. Mepps and gold Cyclones should take a few fish, but don't expect constant action.

From the west end of the Swiftcurrent Motor Inn parking lot, hike toward Swiftcurrent Pass until you see the lake after 2 easy miles.

170 Fishercap Lake

Location: 12 03 03 084 E 54 08 024 N

Elevation: 6,625 ft

Area: 12 acres

Species: EBT/C

The lake offers poor fishing for 8-inch brook trout but is very easy to reach. The shallow bottom and still water make for relatively unproductive water. Most anglers hike farther to Red Rock or Bullhead Lakes. You might think about fishing the stream above or below the lake instead. The willows make it hard to get around the lake, and waders are a must. A small Adams or mosquito pattern in early July should take a couple of fish if fished patiently and gently on the calm surface near the inlet or outlet.

From the west end of the Swiftcurrent Motor Inn parking lot, hike toward Swiftcurrent Pass until you see Fishercap Lake through the trees to the left after just 0.2 mile. You don't see a lot of people fishing this lake; most move on to Red Rock Lake .

171 Iceberg Lake

172 Unnamed Lake (Below Mount Wilbur)

173 Wilbur Creek

Location: 12 03 03 088 E 54 08 032 N

Length: 4.2 miles

Species: EBT/R

174 Ptarmigan Lake

Location: 12 03 01 130 E 54 13 324 N

Elevation: 6,625 ft

Area: 7 acres

Species: RT/C

Ptarmigan Lake harbors non-native fish, which give it something in common with the rest of the Many Glacier area above Sherburne Dam. All nearby waters contain artificially introduced fish populations. However, for some reason Ptarmigan Lake's non-native rainbows got more attention than other self-sustaining introduced populations, and in 1999 there was talk of poisoning the lake to remove the non-native rainbows. After that brief discussion and several angry letters to the editor in the *Hungry Horse News,* the plan lost steam. Notably, these types of aggressive human re-intervention have met with controversy.

Ptarmigan Lake is accessible and the fish are catchable. Hike 4.1 miles from the Iceberg Lake Trailhead behind Swiftcurrent Motor Inn. Turn right after Ptarmigan Falls and watch for a lake before the tunnel.

175 Swiftcurrent Lake

Location: 12 03 04 973 E 54 08 364 N

Elevation: 4,878 ft

Area: 106 acres

Species: EBT/C, KS/R

Even though Swiftcurrent Lake is right next to Many Glacier Hotel and all the tourist traffic in the world, it still has good fishing for brook trout and Kokanee. You can rent a canoe at the hotel and use it to fish either inlet, but you may not be the only one there. The view of Grinnell Point while fishing is worth it. If you have a partner, consider trolling from your canoe. The fishing can be slow, but the brookies are fat and fun to catch. For flies try drifting a prince nymph, Montana, or hare's ear in the inlet from Fishercap Lake. Use some indicator yarn or putty about 6 feet up the line and watch for a strike. If the fish are rising, fish fine leaders and dry flies. A black-and-yellow Mepps trolled should take a couple of fish. For bait I recommend grubs; Kokanee love grubs trolled on a cowbell rig. They usually hang in about 30 feet of water.

The road follows the northern shore from the hotel, and a trail circles the lake starting from the south end of the hotel. Main access points include Many Glacier Hotel, Grinnell Glacier Trailhead, and the boat dock on the north shore of the lake.

176 Natahki Lake

177 Apikuni Creek

178 Lake Sherburne

Location: 12 03 14 874 E 54 11 215 N
Elevation: 4,788 ft (level varies)

Your view from the Many Glacier Hotel across Swiftcurrent Lake.

Area: 1,398 acres

Species: NP/C, EBT/R

The lake offers slow fishing for large northern pike. It would be best to troll the lake, but getting a boat in it is next to impossible because of the absence of a boat dock and the drastic fluctuation of the water level. This fluctuation prevents the fishery from supporting significant populations of fish other than pike, and the pike mostly hang in the shallow flats near the head of the lake. Work the backwater and shallows with large spoons, green Krocodiles, and red Daredevles.

You can walk down to the shore anyplace along the Many Glacier Access Road after entering the park, but I suggest taking the Cracker Lake Trail to the junction with the horse trail to Cracker Flats (the old Boulder Ridge Trail). It is 1.8 miles from the south end of the upper parking lot at Many Glacier Hotel. Use is light and catch rates low. The lake is best fished before the water level drops too low. *Regulations set by the Blackfeet Fish and Game Department.*

179 Governor Pond

180 Unnamed Lake (Sherburne South Shore Pond)

181 Swiftcurrent Ridge Lake

182 Kennedy Lake

183 Kennedy Creek

Location: 12 03 16 709 E 54 17 302 N

Length: 19.4 miles

Species: BT/R, RT/R, EBT/R

Closed to fishing. Check current regulations.

184 Poia Lake

185 Unnamed Lake (Yellow Mountain Pond)

186 Otatso Lakes

187 Otatso Creek

Location: 12 03 16 862 E 54 21 547 N

Length: 12 miles

Species: BT/C, WCT/R

This tributary of Kennedy Creek leads trout to Slide Lakes. *Closed to fishing to facilitate the recovery of bull trout. Check current regulations.*

188 Slide Lake

Location: 12 03 07 990 E 54 19 841 N

Elevation: 6,030 ft

Area: 39 acres

Species: BT/C, YCT-RT Hybrids/R

Closed to fishing to facilitate the recovery of bull trout. Check current regulations.

189 Lower Slide Lake

Location: 12 03 08 594 E 54 19 991 N

Elevation: 5,987 ft

Area: 13 acres

Species: BT/C, YCT-RT Hybrids/R

Closed to fishing to facilitate the recovery of bull trout. Check current regulations.

190 Lee Creek

Location: 12 03 09 828 E 54 30 269 N

Length: 7.4 miles

Species: BT/R, WCT-TR Hybrids/R

Closed to fishing to facilitate the recovery of bull trout. Check current regulations.

191 Jule Creek

Location: 12 03 08 783 E 54 29 146 N

Length: N/A

Species: BT/R

Closed to fishing to facilitate the recovery of bull trout. Check current regulations.

North Fork of Cut Bank Creek Drainage

192 North Fork of Cut Bank Creek

Location: 12 03 25 591 E 53 86 370 N

Length: 26.7 miles

Species: EBT/C, RT/R, YCT/R

In the quest for good small stream fishing in Glacier National Park, I always try to make Cut Bank Creek seem better fishing than it is. There is something pleasurable about fishing long and hard for a few 8- to 10-inch brook trout. I have been skunked half the times I have fished it, but the other half I have stepped off the trail, thrown in a bitch creek nymph, and taken a fish immediately.

The sections up from the Cut Bank Campground offer challenging fishing for cagey brook trout that stack up under the willows in the deep holes. They are hard to catch in midday, and you should get out in the morning if you can. Try to get at the fish before they set up under the banks for the day. Fish only the deep holes and avoid the runs. Electroshocking studies in the past indicated that the fish are there but are concentrated in the deep holes under the willow overgrown banks.

To fish the creeks and lakes of this valley, take Montana Highway 49 to the junction with Cut Bank Creek Road, 17 miles north of East Glacier. Drive 4 miles over a gravel road to the trailhead next to the Cut Bank Campground. You can car camp and fish your way up to Atlantic Falls, 4.1 miles on a relatively flat trail.

193 Unnamed Lake (Amphitheater Basin)

194 Pitamakan Lake

195 Lake of the Winds

196 Katoya Lake

Location: 12 03 19 189 E 53 77 867 N

Elevation: 6,368 ft

Area: 10 acres

North Fork of Cut Bank Creek Drainage

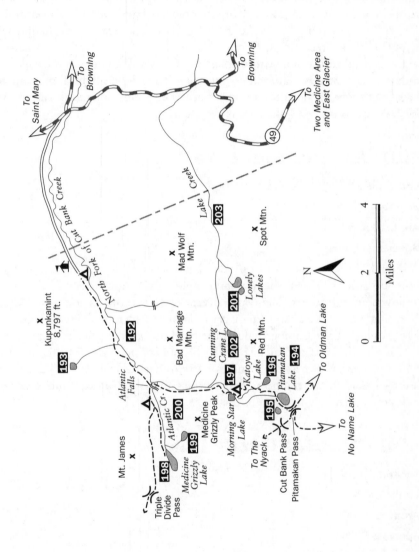

Species: YCT/R

Katoya Lake is hard to get to in June unless you want to walk with snow-shoes. There have been numerous rumors about the size and number of fish. I have visited the lake several times but have never been able to test these rumors. I will tell you that not a lot of people fish it, and it does contain Yellowstone cutthroat trout. The best way to fish this lake is to get a permit to spend a couple of nights at Morning Star Lake and day hike to Katoya.

To reach Morning Star Lake, take Montana Highway 49 to the junction with Cut Bank Creek Road, 17 miles north of East Glacier. Drive 4 miles over a gravel road to the trailhead next to the Cut Bank Campground. Hike 6.6 miles on a relatively flat trail to the lake. Then hike about 1 mile up the Pitamakan Pass Trail until you cross a creek. Follow the creek on an easy bushwhack to Katoya Lake. Use is very light.

197 Morning Star Lake

Location: 12 03 18 786 E 53 79 400 N

Elevation: 5,763 ft

Area: 10 acres

Species: YCT/R

Although this lake once was a productive stocked lake, it suffers from freeze outs because it is so shallow and holds only a sparse population of Yellowstone cutthroats. The water is very clear and the fishing slow. To fish Morning Star, make a day trip or get a permit to spend a couple of nights at Morning Star Lake Campground at the head of the lake, which is a nice spot.

To Reach Morning Star Lake, take Montana Highway 49 to the junction with Cut Bank Creek Road, 17 miles north of East Glacier. Drive 4 miles over a gravel road to the trailhead next to the Cut Bank Campground. Hike 6.6 miles on a relatively flat trail to the lake.

198 Medicine Grizzly Lake

Location: 12 03 16 426 E 53 82 247 N

Elevation: 5,563 ft

Area: 41 acres

Species: RT/C

Medicine Grizzly Lake is better known for its concentrated bear population and false-charging grizzlies than for its fishing. There used to be a camp-ground at the head of the lake, but there were too many bear problems and it was closed and relocated to the most unscenic spot in the park, Atlantic Creek Campground.

The trick to staying in Atlantic Creek Campground is to not stay there

Medicine Grizzly Lake. KIM SCHNEIDER PHOTO

very much. Don't stay in camp except to sleep and cook. Spend your time on Triple Divide Pass Trail or, more appropriately, fishing Medicine Grizzly Lake. The trail is often closed because of bear danger, so I don't recommend you try to carry fish from the lake to the campground. Yellow Mepps, yellow muddlers, and rainbow Cyclones should take a few big rainbows.

The best way to fish this lake is to get a permit to spend a couple of nights at Atlantic Creek Campground, which has no view but does allow fires. To get there, take Montana Highway 49 to the junction with Cut Bank Creek Road, 17 miles north of East Glacier. Drive 4 miles over a gravel road to the trailhead next to the Cut Bank Campground. Hike 4.4 miles on a relatively flat trail, turning toward Triple Divide Pass just before Atlantic Falls to Atlantic Creek Campground. Medicine Grizzly Lake is only 1.8 miles farther in. Medicine Grizzly Lake is lightly fished due to frequent trail closures from false-charging grizzlies, but Atlantic Creek Campground receives lots of non-angler use.

199 Unnamed Lakes (Below Medicine Grizzly Peak)

200 Atlantic Creek

Location: 12 03 19 445 E 53 82 636 N
Length: N/A
Species: EBT/R, RT/R

201 Lonely Lakes

202 Running Crane Lake

203 Lake Creek

Location: 12 03 27 849 E 53 80 130 N
Length: N/A
Species: EBT/R

Two Medicine River Drainage

204 Two Medicine River

Location: 12 03 28 097 E 53 74 343 N

Length: 90.1 miles

Species: EBT/C, RT/R, MWF/R

Two Medicine River generally supports populations of brook trout and rainbow trout. It is best fished outside the park below the reservoir, but a Blackfeet Tribal Permit is required. Above Lower Two Medicine Lake up to Running Eagle Falls, the river offers fair fishing for small brook trout. Access it outside the park or just up- or downstream from the Running Eagle Falls interpretive stop.

205 Lower Two Medicine Lake

Location: 12 03 32 798 E 53 73 283 N

Elevation: 4,882 ft

Area: 718 acres

Species: EBT/C, RT/R

In 1940 John Cook took the state record 9-pound brookie out of Lower Two Medicine Lake. Lower Two Medicine Lake is truly a *lake,* not just a lake created by a reservoir, although the dam at the foot did enlarge the lake somewhat. Your best bet is to wait until the lake lowers and stabilizes, then fish the deeper water near the park border. You need a reservation permit to fish the lower half. For this lake I suggest worm-fishing and beer. Beer always allows you to catch more fish and is essential for any good redneck outing. To access the lake, bushwhack down from the Two Medicine Access Road from East Glacier after you enter the park. *Regulations set by the Blackfeet Fish and Game Department.*

206 Two Medicine Lake

Location: 12 03 25 111 E 53 73 107 N

Elevation: 5,164 ft

Area: 432 acres

Species: EBT/C, RT/R

Like the other lakes in the valley, this one harbors big brookies, but you won't get them in Pray Lake or from the camp store shore. You need to troll from a canoe or float tube, preferably with a leech or bugger. The inlet is hard to fish

Two Medicine River Drainage

x Red Mtn.

213

To Cutbank
Valley

x Mt. Morgan
Oldman
Lake
210   212
Young Man
Lake   211
Boy
Lake

Dawson Pass

No Name
Lake   218

208   209
Upper
Two Medicine
Lake

Dry Fork
215 216   217
Rising
x Wolf   214
Pray L.
Two
Medicine   207
Lake
ferry   206

Sky
L.

T
204   205   Lower
Two Medicine
Lake

Two
Medicine
River

x Scenic Point

49

223

224

Fortymile Creek

To East
Glacier

Two Medicine Creek

Sinopah
Mtn.

Aster Creek
220

Paradise Creek

221

Cobalt
Lake   219

To
Lake
Isabel

222

Appistoki
Creek

x
Appistoki
Peak

x
Mt.
Henry

x
Bison
Mtn.

x
The Head   Midvale Cr.

225

Fortyone Mile Cr.

To
East
Glacier

x
Dancing Lady
Mtn.

Lena
Lake
229

Railroad Creek
226

To East
Glacier

227

Firebrand Pass

To Ole Lake

x
Calf Robe
Mtn.

Green
Lake   231

Lubec
Lake
228

230

Coonsa
Creek

234

T

2

N

0   2   4
Miles

x
Summit
Mtn.

Summit
Lake

Three Bears
Lake
233   232

To
Autumn
Creek

Marias Pass

Summit Creek

234

Park   Boundary

To Essex and
West Glacier

because the boat tours dock there and it is usually shallow and flooded. Paradise Point on the south shore is a good bet for a few fish. Be careful of high winds when floating. For flies try Adams irresistible and Prince nymphs. For lures try rainbow Cyclones, elk hair rooster tails, and yellow Mepps. You can hike around either side of the lake from the Two Medicine Camp Store or rent a canoe from the boat company. A boat ramp near the camp shore offers access to motorized boats with ten horsepower or less.

207 Pray Lake

Location: 12 03 25 265 E 53 73 405 N
Elevation: 5,163 ft
Length: 9 acres
Species: EBT/C, RT/R

208 Upper Two Medicine Lake

Location: 12 03 19 220 E 53 70 855 N
Elevation: 5,551 ft
Area: 155 acres
Species: EBT/C

The largest fish I know of being caught in Upper Two Medicine Lake was an 8-pound brook trout caught just before ice-off between cracks in the ice by

Upper Two Medicine Lake. ERIC HANSON PHOTO

Randy Gayner in the early 1990s. The reality of fishing Upper Two Medicine Lake during most of the summer is crowds, wind, and a few 8- to 12-inch brookies, unless you get to the far end of the lake. For flies try an elk hair caddis off one of the points down the north side of the lake or fish an Adams irresistible in a wind-protected bay. Lure-fishing can be productive, but you need to get away from the shallow outlet and into deeper water.

Access the lake by taking the boat across Two Medicine Lake, then hiking 2 miles to the upper lake. Don't be surprised if you get to tag along on a ranger-led hike. You can camp at the lake, but you can't have a full day to fish because of a one-night stay limit on the campground. Most use concentrates at the foot of the lake, where the campground is also located. The campground receives many non-angling visitors. Many day hikers also try to fish the lake.

209 Unnamed Lake (Upper Two Medicine Pond)

Location: 12 03 19 591 E 53 71 008 N

Elevation: 5,410 ft

Area: N/A

Species: EBT/R

If the big lake is too windy, try this shallow pond below.

210 Oldman Lake

Location: 12 03 18 674 E 53 75 738 N

Elevation: 6,646 ft

Area: 43 acres

Species: YCT/C

In the quest for large, lanky Yellowstone cutthroat and a hell of a workout carrying in your raft or float tube, Oldman Lake is your destination. Long known for good but challenging fishing, Oldman Lake is also located in one of the most picturesque basins in the park. These factors make it a popular destination for hikers and anglers alike, so don't expect to have it to yourself during peak season.

During midday there are not many rises on the surface, and using wet line from a float tube or from the west shore is advised. Trolling a leech from your float tube is a good way to take large cutthroat. A yellow muddler is a deadly Yellowstone cutthroat fly when fished deep. For lures your best bet is to get away from the beach at the east end of the lake where the trail goes down to the shore. It is easiest to work your way around the north shore toward the inlet and cast out into deep water, letting your lure sink several seconds before

Oldman Lake from Rising Wolf. KIM SCHNEIDER PHOTO

retrieving it. You also may be able to pick up a couple of fish from the stream below the lake on dry flies. The lake is best fished after July 15.

Access the lake by hiking 6.8 miles from the Two Medicine Campground; the trailhead is located near Pray Lake on the paved loop. The hike is gradual but long enough to make day trips with a float tube difficult. Oldman Lake is fished regularly, but quite a few anglers get skunked.

211 Young Man Lake

212 Boy Lake

213 Unnamed Lake (Below Red Mountain)

214 Sky Lake

215 Unnamed Lake (Below Rising Wolf #1)

216 Unnamed Lake (Below Rising Wolf #2)

217 Dry Fork

Location: 12 03 26 486 E 53 74 061 N

Length: 4.5 miles

Species: YCT/R, BT/R

This steep cascading stream holds a few fish around Oldman Lake, but is otherwise pretty void of fish.

218 No Name Lake

Location: 12 03 19 342 E 53 72 267 N

Elevation: 5,925 ft

Area: 10 acres

Species: EBT/C, RT/C

No Name Lake contains small rainbows and brookies that will feed vigorously when food is on the water. The lake is small and has a limited food supply, so don't expect fat fish. The campground at the head of the lake allows easy access to the inlet, which offers good fishing.

From the Two Medicine Lake Boat Dock, hike just under 2 miles toward Dawson Pass to No Name Lake. Most of the overnight visitors are through-hikers, but the lake does receive some day angling pressure.

219 Cobalt Lake

220 Aster Creek

221 Paradise Creek

Location: 12 03 24 290 E 53 72 240 N
Length: 6.1 miles
Species: EBT/R, RT/R

222 Appistoki Creek

223 Fortymile Creek

Location: 12 03 33 012 E 53 73 055 N
Length: N/A
Species: EBT/R

224 Fortyone Mile Creek

Location: 12 03 33 518 E 53 71 983 N
Length: N/A
Species: EBT/R

225 Midvale Creek

Location: 12 03 35 887 E 53 67 326 N (East Glacier)
Length: 11.2 miles
Species: EBT/C, MWF/R

226 Railroad Creek

Location: 12 03 33 977 E 53 63 560 N
Length: 9.1 miles
Species: EBT/C, MWF/R

227 Unnamed Lake (South Fork of Railroad Creek)

228 Lubec Lake

229 Lena Lake

230 Coonsa Creek

Location: 12 03 32 479 E 53 58 488 N
Length: 3.6 miles
Species: EBT/R

This tributary of Summit Creek may hold a few brookies.

231 Green Lake

This lake appears to have no natural barriers to brook trout exploitation of its waters.

232 Summit Lake

Location: 12 03 25 765 E 53 55 447 N
Elevation: 5,200 ft
Area: N/A
Species: EBT/R, MWF/R, WCT-RT Hybrids/R, WCT/R

233 Three Bears Lake

Three Bears Lake may not have any fish, and the man-made earthen road on the west end probably will keep it that way. Scientists think this may have been the location of indigenous westslope cutthroat crossing the Continental

Divide, similar to the migration of Yellowstone cutthroat trout across the Two Ocean Plateau above Yellowstone Lake.

234 Summit Creek

Location: 12 03 31 480 E 53 58 392 N

Length: 4.2 miles

Species: EBT/C, MWF/R, WCT-RT Hybrids/R, WCT/R

Middle Fork of the Flathead River Drainage

235 Middle Fork of the Flathead River

Location: 12 03 09 445 E 53 45 213 N (Bear Creek) 11 07 16 611 E 53 71 973 N (Blankenship)

Length: 92 miles

Species: MWF/C, WCT/C, BT/R, RT/R, EBT/R, LT/R

The Middle Fork of the Flathead River is probably better known for its rapids than for its fishing, but many anglers get the chance to fish it because of the easy access from U.S. Highway 2 and the four rafting companies that float it. It provides a little less action than the North Fork but has a similar number of 8- to 10-inch cutthroat as well as bigger rainbows and a few lake trout. Later in the season most of the pressure is concentrated in the canyon section just before West Glacier.

The Middle Fork of the Flathead River forms the southern and western boundary of Glacier National Park. Technically the border is the high water mark on the park side, and consequently a Montana fishing license is required for all river fishing. You should be able to catch a few small cutthroats on almost any stretch of the river between Bear Creek and the confluence with the North Fork at Blankenship Bridge. When the fish are feeding, the action is pretty constant, including a few big rainbows and cutt-bows. When the river is muddy, remember to fish the shallow water. Check above Coal Creek, because most of the silt usually comes out of the Coal and Pinchot Creeks area that burned in 1983.

The Middle Fork marked the epicenter of the infamous 1964 flood. On an annual basis, the Middle Fork averages a discharge of less than 3,000 cubic feet per second (cfs), but on June 9, 1964, the river gushed 140,000 cfs and scoured its streambed so badly that the results will be obvious for years to come. Fortunately, such a flood should occur only once in about 200 years.

The Middle Fork is a nutrient poor but exceptionally clean waterway. Unfortunately, because of this it does not support populations of big fish like the famous tailwater fisheries in Montana such as the Missouri. The fish need to eat everything they can to survive and do not have the luxury of picking only the most efficient, nutrient-rich foods. The cutthroat average less than 12 inches, occasionally reaching 16 to 20 inches. They will take most stimulator patterns if presented without drag. Some bigger lake trout have moved up from Flathead Lake to feed on the cutthroats that the bull trout used to eat. The numbers of bull trout spawning in Middle Fork tributaries were up significantly in 2000, and anglers should keep their fingers crossed

A 1964 flood washed away everything but the cement arch of the old bridge that crosses the Middle Fork above West Glacier.

for recovery and the eventual reopening of catch-and-release fishing for bull trout throughout the drainage.

For flies I recommend yellow humpy, parachute Adams, olive woolly bugger, black woolly worm, Chernobyl hoppers, nonstandard ties of orange, yellow, and green stimulators, bead-head pheasant tail, and Prince nymphs. For lures I recommend red-and-silver spoon patterns and elk hair rooster tails. Remember to cut off at least the third treble hook for catch-and-release. Fish the deep holes closer to the top earlier in the year and move toward the tails later in the summer.

Access on the park side is via the boundary trail, which follows the river from West Glacier to Walton Ranger Station. U.S. Highway 2 follows the south side of the river for its entire course, with river access sites at Bear Creek, Essex, Paola, Cascadilla, Moccasin Creek, and West Glacier. You can also hike down from the highway in several spots. This is especially common in the whitewater section of John Stevens Canyon, where deep green holes beckon the auto tourist from above. Several spots on the upper river between Bear Creek and Cascadilla offer access along less-visited stretches, but if you can see it from the highway so can everybody else. Heaviest use is concentrated on the John Stevens Canyon section between the Moccasin Creek River Access and West Glacier. Use on the upper stretch of the river decreases as the water level drops and it becomes unfloatable. Peak use is from July through late August. The drainage is best fished after June, when the upper river starts to clear up.

Middle Fork of the Flathead River Drainage

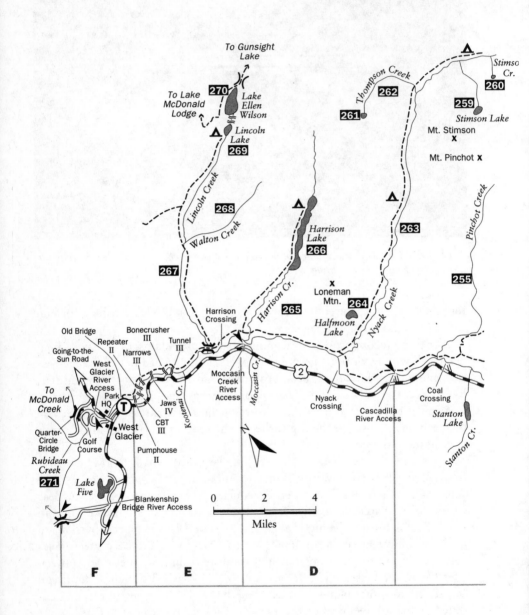

Middle Fork of the Flathead River Drainage

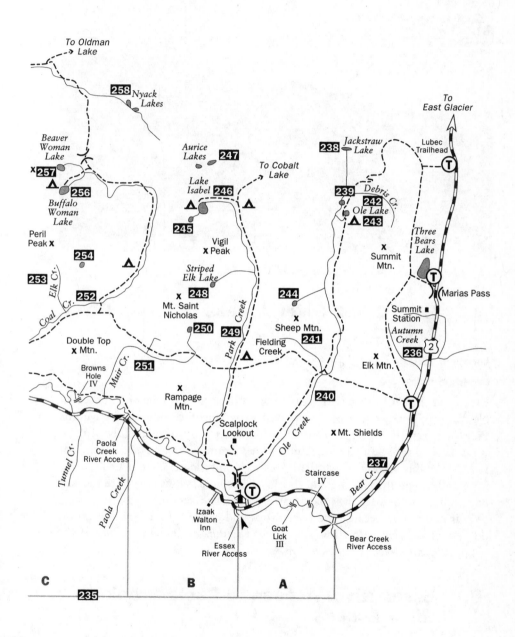

To Oldman Lake

258 Nyack Lakes

To East Glacier

Beaver Woman Lake

Jackstraw Lake

238

Lubec Trailhead

Ⓣ

X 257

Aurice Lakes

247

△ 256

Lake Isabel 246

To Cobalt Lake

Buffalo Woman Lake

239

Debris Cr.

242

Ole Lake

△ 243

Three Bears Lake

Peril Peak X

254

△ 245

Vigil X Peak

X Summit Mtn.

Ⓣ

Marias Pass

253

Striped Elk Lake

Summit Station

252

X 248

Mt. Saint Nicholas

244

Autumn Creek

Coal Cr.

Elk Cr.

X 250

249

X Sheep Mtn.

236 2

Double Top X Mtn.

Park Creek

△ Fielding Creek

241

X Elk Mtn.

Browns Hole IV

251

Muir Cr.

X Rampage Mtn.

Ⓣ

240

X Mt. Shields

Paola Creek River Access

Scalplock Lookout

237

Bear Cr.

Tunnel Cr.

Paola Creek

Ole Creek

Staircase IV

Ⓣ

Izaak Walton Inn

Goat Lick III

Bear Creek River Access

Essex River Access

C

235

B

A

Fall fishing in the shadows of Loneman Lookout. KIM SCHNEIDER PHOTO

A. Bear Creek River Access to Essex River Access

Location: 12 03 09 445 E 53 45 213 N (Bear Creek)

Length: 5 miles

Except for the confluence with Bear Creek, this section is relatively inaccessible from the road, but it offers the best early-season fishing on the Middle Fork. It is very floatable in a raft or whitewater dory through July in most years. Several rapids, including Dump Truck (Staircase on the map) and Goat Lick, make this section too difficult for beginning floaters. Goat Lick makes for excellent wildlife viewing and there is a nice hole below, but we're focused on fishing, so don't let the goats distract you. The action on this stretch of river is good early because the river drops and clears before peak season on the rest of the river. *No fishing is allowed within a 100-yard radius of the mouth of Bear Creek. Check current regulations.*

B. Essex River Access to Paola Creek River Access

Location: 12 03 06 771 E 53 49 892 N (Essex)

Length: 8 miles

This is one of the more away-from-the-road sections of the river. This section holds about twice as many whitefish as it does cutthroat but seems to produce some bigger fish than other sections above. Fishing with your favorite bead-head nymph should produce plenty of whitefish, and a parachute Adams or green stimulator should take a few cutthroats. The population also benefits from feeder-rearing streams like Park Creek, which, although closed to fishing, help produce some bigger fish that mature and move into the main river.

C. Paola Creek River Access to Cascadilla River Access

Location: 12 03 04 359 E 53 57 725 N (Paola)

Length: 11 miles

Some of these sections of the river are eroded layers of clay that get swept clean every spring and don't hold fish, but in between are some deep holes that do hold fish. On the lower stretches, especially after the burn area, you can fish deep for lake trout that have moved up from Flathead Lake. Some good spots to walk are down at Stanton Creek and up from the Paola Creek access to the inlet of Paola Creek. Remember, Brown's Hole, a sometimes close-to-Class V rapid, haunts this section, but it is only extreme at around 5.5 feet above low water at the West Glacier Bridge. By the time the water clears for fishing, the main obstacle to floaters is the rock garden just above Brown's Hole, tricky for even the most experienced floaters.

Steep shale walls characterize the Middle Fork of the Flathead between Paola River Access and Cascadilla River Access.

D. Cascadilla River Access to Moccasin Creek River Access

Location: 12 02 94 732 E 53 67 083 N

Length: 8 miles

Don't try floating this section until the water drops a bit in July; the channel changes every year and the flats are filled with logjams and other hazards. For me, floating through root balls, sweepers, and logs everywhere evokes a ghost-like melancholy about accidents past. Please use caution.

This is probably the slowest section of the river, mostly because the Nyack Flats get scoured every spring and few permanent ripples last more than a year or two. One deep hole is where Nyack Creek enters the river. The fish may be picky here, but there are some big ones in the deeps. You can't fish Nyack Creek, so this is the only chance to taste what it might be like if bull trout populations recover enough to warrant reopening Nyack Creek to fishing. The fishing becomes a little more active as you approach Moccasin Creek. Wade Moccasin Creek and walk across the island from the put-in to fish the lower stretch.

E. Moccasin Creek River Access to West Glacier River Access

Location: 12 02 89 671 E 53 73 400 N (Moccasin)

Length: 8 miles

This heavily trafficked section of river also has fish. Later in the year terrestrials and smaller spoons will take cutthroat and cutt-bows in the deep canyon holes. So many rafts float this section of river that the fish are very used to boats and are not easily spooked. The area at the old bridge above West Glacier is fished pretty heavily. At Bone Crusher rapid, where the photographers take pictures of rafters, you can sometimes catch fish in between rafts with an audience. Another place that is heavily fished on this section but often produces fish is the Jaws hole, but if you drop your fly box in the water I don't recommend pursuing it.

F. West Glacier River Access to Blankenship Bridge River Access

Location: 12 02 78 966 E 53 76 505 N (West Glacier) 11 07 16 611 E 53 71 973 N (Blankenship)

Length: 6 miles

This calm section of river is more productive than many might think. Local outfitters fish it heavily. The Quarter-Circle Bridge where McDonald Creek

Fewer, but larger, native westslope cutthroats can be found in Nyack Flats between Cascadilla River Access and Moccasin Creek River Access. KIM SCHNEIDER PHOTO

enters is a good place for a patient angler to sit for a while. The cutthroat and rainbows in the section between the river and the lake see a lot of flies, so you might have to resort to small flies to get a rise. There are several productive riffles just before the canyon, where the deep water and hydraulics make presentation of a fly difficult but lures efficient. Late in the season, before Blankenship Bridge, the whitefish and bigger rainbows will begin to hit terrestrials like hoppers and crickets. For whitefish, a small bead-head on a sink tip line in the deep holes should bring in the harvest.

236 Autumn Creek

Location: 12 03 21 010 E 53 51 375 N

Length: 16.2 miles

Species: WCT/C, BT/R

This tributary of Bear Creek makes for a nice day hike or winter cross-country ski, but it's not much for fishing.

237 Bear Creek

Location: 12 03 09 445 E 53 45 213 N

Length: 16.2 miles

Species: WCT/C, BT/R, MWF/R

This tributary of the Middle Fork is rarely fished and in places awfully scarred by the straightening of U.S. Highway 2. However, being near a road has its advantages, and on your way to or from fishing a quick stop to give pan-sized cutthroats some exercise may be in order. Focus on sections less straightened by the road. Fish concentrate in the pools, not in the runs.

238 Jackstraw Lake

239 Unnamed Lake (Upper Ole Creek)

240 Ole Creek

Location: 12 03 07 246 E 53 50 722 N

Length: 16.2 miles

Species: WCT/C, MWF/C, BT/R

Closed to fishing to facilitate the recovery of bull trout. Check current regulations.

241 Fielding Creek

Location: 12 03 15 438 E 53 53 276 N

Length: 2 miles

Species: WCT/C

Closed to fishing to facilitate the recovery of bull trout. Check current regulations.

242 Debris Creek

Location: 12 03 24 316 E 53 62 585 N

Length: N/A

Species: WCT/C

Closed to fishing to facilitate the recovery of bull trout. Check current regulations.

243 Ole Lake

Location: 12 03 23 566 E 53 61 164 N

Elevation: 5,535 ft

Area: 5 acres

Species: WCT/A

Ole Lake is a great place to learn to fish, especially if you want to take your son or daughter there for a first fishing experience. The fish are small but very easy to catch. A starved cutthroat population allowed one angler to catch-and-release more than 40 fish in one hour. The fishing is not always that good, but it is the closest thing to a sure bet I know.

Ole Lake is not more than 10 feet deep in almost the entire lake, so it is a wonder that the fish don't die of winterkill. It is easy to see why they are so hungry. A healthy mosquito population provides a meager diet for the cutthroat in this small lake. The fish average 6 to 8 inches, with a stretch for a 10-inch or longer fish. It is sometimes hard to tell if you keep catching the same fish unless you tag them, but I don't recommend it. The only strategy I have for this lake is to tie a semi-descent knot and put on your favorite fly or lure. From my experience the Green Giant™ (corn) is also very effective.

Access the lake via Firebrand Pass on the Ole Lake Trail, which starts at mile marker 203 on U.S. Highway 2. Hike 7.7 miles in on a well-maintained trail; the hike back out is much tougher. A backcountry permit is required to camp at Ole Lake. There are only two tent sites at Ole Lake, so it is extremely unlikely you will ever see more than eight people there, and other than late July and early August, you will likely be the only ones there.

244 Unnamed Lake (Below Brave Dog Mountain)

245 Upper Lake Isabel

Location: 12 03 14 644 E 53 65 928 N

Elevation: 5,990 ft

Area: 15 acres

Species: WCT/C, BT/C

Oddly enough, in Lake Isabel and Upper Lake Isabel, bull trout and cutthroat trout are both small and hungry, and often the cutthroat are bigger. The FWP *Bull Trout Status Report* also indicates that to date, "no bull trout larger than 12 inches have been collected from either lake." However, the cutthroats don't get much bigger either. Although a little culling of the herd would not likely harm these populations, remember to carefully identify your catch and remember too, that all bull trout must be carefully released. After fishing the lower lake, you may realize that the fishing will be just as good in the upper lake.

246 Lake Isabel

Location: 12 03 15 853 E 53 66 170 N

Elevation: 5,715 ft

Area: 43 acres

Species: WCT/C, BT/C

Lake Isabel is one of the most beautiful and hard to reach lakes in the park. It is well known for its fishing, but it can get a little boring catching fish on every cast. Almost all the fish are exactly the same size, stunted by a limited food supply and the excess number of fish. Despite this overpopulation, remember to carefully identify your catch and remember too, that all bull trout must be carefully released.

On one memorable fishing trip, after an extensive amount of hiking, I reached Lake Isabel and was anxious to get a line in the water, but as I was tying on my fly and watching several cruising trout I realized that they were fighting over the sunflower seeds floating on the water. After I finished rigging my line they were fighting over my fly. After catching twenty or thirty 10- to 13-inch, all-head cutthroats, my brother and I got a little bored and decided to see if the fish would take anything, even the dreaded big green frog imitation. Some fish would be scared of this metal-painted, green-haired fly, but not a Lake Isabel trout.

Access either Upper Lake Isabel or Lake Isabel by either hiking the long, flat, forested Park Creek Trail from Walton Ranger Station or making the grueling climb over Two Medicine Pass from Two Medicine Lake. At 16.9 and 15.3 miles respectively, both routes are less than doable in a day for a normal person.

247 Aurice Lakes

248 Striped Elk Lake

This lake is rumored to have fish, but it is a tough rumor to prove or disprove. Anyone who makes it there deserves to know and has earned the right not to tell anybody.

249 Park Creek

Location: 12 03 06 252 E 53 53 800 N

Length: 14.4 miles

Species: WCT/C, MWF/C, BT/R

Closed to fishing to facilitate the recovery of bull trout. Check current regulations.

250 Unnamed Lake (Salvage Basin)

251 Muir Creek

Location: 12 03 03 673 E 53 60 024 N

Length: 7.8 miles

Species: WCT/C, BT/C

Closed to fishing to facilitate the recovery of bull trout. Check current regulations.

252 Coal Creek

Location: 12 02 98 169 E 53 66 296 N

Length: 15.7 miles

Species: WCT/C, BT/C

Closed to fishing to facilitate the recovery of bull trout. Check current regulations.

253 Elk Creek

Location: 12 03 06 820 E 53 65 094 N

Length: 5.3 miles

Species: WCT/R

This tributary of Coal Creek grows a few small cutthroat. *Closed to fishing to facilitate the recovery of bull trout. Check current regulations.*

254 Unnamed Lake (Below Cloudcroft Peak)

255 Pinchot Creek

Location: 12 03 00 281 E 53 66 519 N

Length: 8.9 miles

Species: WCT/C, BT/C

Closed to fishing to facilitate the recovery of bull trout. Check current regulations.

256 Buffalo Woman Lake

257 Beaver Woman Lake

258 Nyack Lakes

These lakes may have been planted historically but are not known to contain fish. *Check current regulations.*

259 Stimson Lake

260 Unnamed Lake (Stimson Creek)

261 Unnamed Lakes (Thompson Lakes #1 & #2)

262 Thompson Creek

263 Nyack Creek

Location: 12 02 92 886 E 53 70 486 N

Length: 24 miles

Species: WCT/C, BT/C

Closed to fishing to facilitate the recovery of bull trout. Check current regulations.

264 Halfmoon Lake

265 Harrison Creek

Location: 12 02 89 349 E 53 74 289 N

Length: 4.5 miles

Species: EBT/C, WCT/C, RBT/R, BT/R, MWF/C

266 Harrison Lake

Location: 12 02 93 809 E 53 74 289 N

Elevation: 3,693 ft

Area: 412 acres

Species: MWF/A, WCT/C, BT/C, LT/C, EBT/C, RBT/R, KS/R

This little-visited, hard to reach lake offers solitude and a variety of possible fish in your creel. Brook trout and lake trout are both common here. Make sure to eat a few of them during your stay. Harrison Lake was once well known for its large rainbows. It still has some big fish and lots of cutthroat from the river. The fishing is off-and-on and the only real place to cast is the inlet. You can solve this problem by carrying that heavy float tube or raft. Don't expect too much of a view, though. The hike in and the campsite are in the trees, and the Boundary Trail from Lincoln Lake Trail to Harrison Lake

Harrison Lake

Trail is almost completely overgrown. The waters of Harrison Lake heat up in the summer, and fish hang out near the cool waters of the inlet, mostly feeding wet on dead drifted nymphs. Try a stimulator pattern or a parachute Adams up the creek, but be careful not to spook the fish.

To access the lake from West Glacier, hike the Boundary Trail for 7.1 miles, then join the Harrison Lake Trail for another 2.9 miles. To shorten this trip in late season, ford the Middle Fork of the Flathead and follow a cross-country route to the Boundary Trail. The best place to do this is on a railroad access road 0.5 mile west of Moccasin Creek River Access. Use is light. Harrison Lake does not receive many visitors except during the peak season when permits are hard to get, so this is one of your better opportunities for having a lake all to yourself.

267 Lincoln Creek

Location: 12 02 89 755 E 53 81 240 N

Length: 9.7 miles

Species: WCT/A, EBT/R, BT/R, MWF/R

Lincoln Creek contains small cutthroats and is not an easy day trip without crossing the Middle Fork.

268 Walton Creek

Location: 12 02 89 755 E 53 81 240 N

Length: 6.7 miles

Species: WCT/A, EBT/R, BT/R, MWF/R

This tributary of Lincoln Creek is rarely fished and provides training grounds for future Middle Fork cutthroats.

269 Lincoln Lake

Location: 12 02 95 464 E 53 85 231 N

Elevation: 4,598 ft

Area: 37 acres

Species: WCT/C, BT/R, EBT/R

Lincoln Lake gets fresh water from Lake Ellen Wilson via a cliffside waterfall. The cliff and the lack of a trail prevent hiking from one to the other, but Lincoln Lake offers good fishing for westslope cutthroats. The cutthroats in Lincoln Lake are numerous and range from 8 to 16 inches. There are some resident bull trout. The outlet and the inlet both fish well. A gray Wulff and a gold Thomas Cyclone should be effective.

The Lincoln Lake Trail starts on Going-to-the-Sun Road 1.5 miles west of Lake McDonald Lodge at a well-marked trailhead. It is an 8-mile, mostly uphill trek over the ridge to Lincoln Lake. During peak season Lincoln Lake receives heavy visitation because of its proximity to Lake McDonald Lodge and Going-to-the-Sun Road.

270 Lake Ellen Wilson

Location: 12 02 96 648 E 53 85 962 N

Elevation: 5,929 ft

Area: 211 acres

Species: EBT/C

This brook trout–filled lake is an excellent stop on a Gunsight–Lake Ellen Wilson backpack trip. The peaks and the large boulder near the campground offer a pleasant setting to catch a few fish and take a few naps. The inlet right at the campground is a good place to try. This is one lake where spin-fishing might prove more successful than fly-fishing. If you have a lot of energy, hike around to the east end of the lake by the cliffs and fish a silver spoon deep.

To reach Lake Ellen Wilson, I suggest planning a three-day backpack trip from Jackson Glacier Overlook to Lake McDonald Lodge. Stay at Gunsight Lake and fish the first night; climb Gunsight Pass and fish Lake Ellen Wilson the second night. There is heavy hiker use but rather spotty fishing pressure. Ellen Wilson has one campground with four sites. It is unlikely that more than a few hikers will fish.

271 Rubideau Creek

Waterfall drop into the Middle Fork canyon between West Glacier and Blankenship makes for a pretty site and a pretty impassable barrier to upstream proliferation.

Resources

Glacier Natural History Association
P.O. Box 310
West Glacier, MT 59936
(406) 888–5756
gnha@glacierassociation.org

Glacier National Park
P.O. Box 128
West Glacier, MT 59936
(406) 888–7800 (voice)
(406) 888–7896 (TDD)
www.nps.gov/glac
glac_info@nps.gov

Montana Fish Wildlife & Parks-
REGION 1
490 North Meridian Road
Kalispell, MT 59901
(406) 752–5501
fwprg1@state.mt.us
fwp.state.mt.us

Travel Montana
P.O. Box 7549
Missoula, MT 59807-7549
(406) 444–2654 (in MT)
(800) VISIT–MT (outside MT)
www.travel.state.mt.us

USGS
U.S. Department of the Interior
U.S. Geological Survey
12201 Sunrise Valley Drive
Reston, VA 20192
mapping.usgs.gov

Waterton National Park
Waterton Park, Alberta
Canada T0K 2MO
(403) 859–2224
waterton_info@pch.gc.ca
parkscanada.pch.gc.ca/waterton/

Guided Backpacking Concessionaire and Float Trips on Middle and North Forks of the Flathead River

Glacier Wilderness Guides
P.O. Box 330
West Glacier, MT 59936
(406) 387–5555
www.glacierguides.com
glguides@cyberport.net

Boat Tour Concessionaire

Glacier Park Boat Company
P.O. Box 5262
Kalispell, MT 59903
(406) 257–2426
gpboats@montanaweb.com
www.montanaweb.com/gpboats

Waterton Boat Tour/Shuttle to Goat Haunt

Waterton Inter-Nation Shoreline
Cruise Co. Ltd.
P.O. Box 126
Waterton, Alberta
Canada T0K 2M0
(403) 859–2362

Lodging and Visitor Services Concessionaire

Glacier Park Inc.
Reservations:
106 Cooperative Way, Suite 104
Kalispell, MT 59901
(406) 756–2444 (year-round)
info@glacierparkinc.com
www.glacierparkinc.com

Glacier Area Fishing Suppliers

Glacier Park Trading Co.
U.S. Highway 2
East Glacier, MT
(406) 226–4433

Glacier Raft Company and Fly Shop
P.O. Box 210 C
West Glacier, MT 59936
(800) 235–6781
(406) 888–5454
grc@glacierraftco.com
www.glacierraftco.com

Park Cafe and Grocery
St. Mary, MT 59417
(406) 732–4482

St. Mary Lodge and Resort
St. Mary, MT 59417
(406) 732–4431
(800) 368–3689
stmary@glcpark.com
www.glcpark.com

West Glacier Mercantile
P.O. Box 398
West Glacier, MT 59936
(406) 888–5403
lodging@westglacier.com

Select Bibliography

Angler Volunteer Censusing Summary. West Glacier, Mont.: United States Fish and Wildlife Service, 1982.

Brown, C. J. D., Dr. *Fishes of Montana*. Bozeman, Mont.: Big Sky Books and Endowment and Research Foundation at Montana State University, 1971.

Bukantis, Robert. "Mysis: Friend or Foe?" *Yellow Bay Journal*, No. 1 (Fall 1986): 1, 12–14

Canadian Wildlife Service of the National Parks Branch. *Anglers' Guide to Canada's Mountain National Parks*. Ottawa: Canada Government Travel Bureau, 1954.

Fishing the Flathead. West Glacier, Mont.: Glacier Natural History Association, Mont., n.d.

Fredenberg, Wade. Unpublished netting survey of west-side lakes in Glacier National Park, 2000.

Glacier Backcountry Camping Guide. United States Department of Interior, National Park Service, 2000.

Glacier Fishing Regulations. United States Department of Interior, National Park Service, 1999–2000.

Glacier National Park Fish Species. United States Department of Interior, National Park Service, 1997.

Hafele, Rick, and Dave Hughes. *The Complete Book of Western Hatches*. Portland, Oreg. : Frank Amato Publications, 1981.

Hintzen, Paul. *Fishing Glacier National Park*. West Glacier: Glacier Natural History Association, 1992.

Holterman, Jack. *Place Names of Waterton–Glacier National Park*. West Glacier: Glacier Natural History Association, 1985.

Hooked for Good, Hooked for Life: The Passion for Fishing the Belly River. Kalispell, Mont.: Life Preservers, 1998.

"Impacts of Hatchery Stocks on Wild Fish Populations." In *Fish Culture in Fisheries Management*, edited by R. H. Stroud, 339–47. Bethesda, Md.: American Fishing Society, 1986.

Kinnie, Ernest J. *Fishing Guide to Glacier National Park*. Berkeley: Gazette Press, 1960.

Marnell, L. F. "Fossil Zooplankton and the Historical Status of the Westslope Cutthroat Trout in a Headwater Lake of Glacier National Park,

Montana." In *Transactions of the American Fisheries Society,* No. 126. Bethesda, Md: American Fishing Society, 1997.

McClung, Brian. *Belly River's Famous Joe Cosley.* Kalispell, Mont.: Life Preservers, 1998.

Molvar, Erik. *Hiking Glacier and Waterton Lakes National Parks.* Helena, Mont.: Falcon Publishing, 1994.

Montana Fishing Regulations. Helena, Mont.: Montana Department of Fish, Wildlife and Parks, 2000.

Moylan, Bridget E. *Glacier's Grandest: A Pictorial History of the Hotels and Chalets of Glacier National Park.* Missoula, Mont.: Pictorial Histories Publishing Company, 1995.

National Park Digital Guide: Glacier National Park. Greenland, N.H.: Maptech, 1998.

Schultz, Leonard P. *Fishes of Glacier National Park, Montana.* United States Department of the Interior, Conservation Bulletin No. 22. Washington, D.C.: U.S. Government Printing Office, 1941.

"Status of the Westslope Cutthroat Trout in Glacier National Park, Montana." In *Biology and Management of the Interior Cutthroat Trout,* edited by R. E. Gresswell, 61–70. Symposium No. 4. Bethesda, Md.: American Fishing Society, 1988.

Three Forks of the Flathead River: Floating Guide. West Glacier: Glacier Natural History Association. n.d.

United States Department of Interior Geological Survey Glacier National Park. Denver, Colo.: United States Geological Survey, 1968.

Index

A

Agassiz Creek, 42-43
Akaiyan Lake, 87
Akokala Creek, 44
Akokala Lake, 44
Allen Creek, 105
Anaconda Creek, 54
Anaconda Lake, 54
Apgar Creek, 83
Apikuni Creek, 110
Appistoki Creek, 125
arctic grayling, 25
Arrow Lake, 57
Aster Creek, 125
Atlantic Creek, 118
Atsina Lake, 74
Aurice Lakes, 139
Autumn Creek, 136
Avalanche Creek, 88
Avalanche Lake, 88–89
avoiding crowds, 16–17

B

backcountry permits, 1, 7, 9
bait fishing, 15
Baring Creek, 100
bears, 1, 9
Bear Creek River Access, 132
Bear Creek, 136
Beaver Woman Lake, 140
Belly River Drainage, 70–79
Belly River, 1, 13
Belly River, 70, 73–74
Bench Lake, 68
Big Creek River Access, 38–39
Bighorn River, 13
Blackfeet Fish and Game
    Department, 8
Blackfeet Indian Reservation, 3
Blackfeet tribal permits, 8
Blankenship Bridge River Access,
    39, 134, 136

B

Bob Marshall Wilderness, 1
Boulder Creek, 104
Boulder Lakes, 104
Boundary Creek, 65
Bowman Creek, 47–48
Bowman Lake, 46–47
Boy Lake, 124
brook trout, 21
Buffalo Woman Lake, 140
bull trout, 2, 22–23

C

Camas Bridge, 37–38
Camas Creek, 55–56
Camas Lake, 2, 57–58
Cameron Lake, 65
Camp Creek, 66
camping, 1
camping permits, 7, 9
Canadian Boarder River Access, 36
Canyon Creek, 105
Caracajou Lake, 65
Casadilla River Access, 133–34
Cataract Creek, 105
catch-and-release fishing, 1
Cerulean Lake, 50
cleaning fish, 1, 9
Cleveland Creek, 66
Coal Creek, 139–40
Cobalt Lake, 125
Cole Creek River Access, 37
Continental Creek, 91
Coonsa Creek, 126
Cosley Lake, 77
courtesy, 9–10
Cracker Lake, 105
Cummings Creek, 50, 52
cutthroat-rainbow hybrid, 1
cutthroat trout, 2, 15
    western, 29
    Yellowstone, 29–30

D

day-use areas, 1
Debris Creek, 137
Divide Creek, 103–4
Dry Fork, 124
Duck Lake, 3
Dutch Creek, 54
Dutch Lakes, 2, 55

E

Elizabeth Lake, 78–79
Elk Creek, 140
equipment, 19–20
Essex River Access, 132–33

F

Falling Leaf Lake, 105
Feather Woman Lake, 87
Fern Creek, 83
Fielding Creek, 137
finding remote lakes, 4
fish, 21–31
cleaning, 1, 9
eating, 1–2
identifying, 24
native, nonnative, 21, 31
population, 13
stocking, 2–3
threat to, 2
fishing
bait-fishing, 14, 17
catch-and-release, 1
courtesy, 9–10
fly-fishing, 15, 17–18
lure-fishing, 13–14, 17–18
regulations, 7–8
Fish Creek, 83
Fish Lake, 87
Fishercap Lake, 108
fly fishing, 15, 18
Ford Creek, 43
Ford Work Station River Access, 36–37
Fortymile Creek, 125
Fortyone Mile Creek, 125

G

GPS, 4
Glacier National Park, 7
fish of, 21–31
lakes of, 16–18
origin of, 1
rivers of, 13–15
Glacier Natural History Association, 7
Glacier Rim River Access, 39
Glenns Lake, 76
Goat Haunt Lake, 65
Goat Lake, 100
Governor Pond, 111
Grace Lake, 53
Great Northern Flats River Access, 38–39
Green Lake, 126
Grinnell Lake, 106
Gunsight Lake, 98
Gyrfalcon Lake, 50

H

Halfmoon Lake, 141
Harrison Creek, 141
Harrison Lake, 141, 143
Helen Lake, 99
Hidden Creek, 89
Hidden Lake, 90
Hidden Meadow Ponds, 48
hiking regulations, 8–9
Howe Creek, 84
Hudson Creek, 103

I

Iceberg Lake, 108
Ipasha Lake, 74

J

Jackson Creek, 85
Jackstraw Lake, 136
Jefferson Creek, 46
Johns Lake, 87
Jule Creek, 113

K

Kaina Lake, 74
Katoya Lake, 114, 116
Kennedy Creek, 111
Kennedy Lake, 111
Kintla Creek, 41
Kintla Lake, 41–42
Kishenehn Creek, 40
kokanee salmon, 25–26
Kootenai Creek, 68
Kootenai Lakes, 66

L

Lake Creek, 118
Lake Ellen Wilson, 144
Lake Evangeline, 58
Lake Francis, 63–64
Lake Isabel, 17, 138–39
Lake Janet, 64
Lake Josephine, 106
Lake McDonald, 82–83
Lake Nooney, 65
Lake of the Winds, 114
Lake Sherburne, 110–11
lake trout, 15, 23
lake whitefish, 25
Lake Wurdeman, 65
lakes, 16–18
  access, 16–17
number of, 1, 16
  presentation, 18
remote, 4, 16–17
  strategies for fishing, 17–18
lead weights, 8
Lee Creek, 112
Lena Lake, 126
Lincoln Creek, 143
Lincoln Lake, 143
Logan Creek, 90
Logan Pass Visitors Center, 1
Logging Creek, 52
Logging Lake, 52–53
Lonely Lakes, 118
Long Bow Creek, 43
Long Bow Lake, 43
Longfellow Creek, 91

Lost Lake, 100
Lower Bullhead Lake, 107
Lower Howe Lake, 85
Lower Quartz Lake, 48–49
Lower Slide Lake, 112
Lower Snyder Lake, 88
Lower Two Medicine Lake, 119
Lubec Lake, 126
lures, 13–14, 18

M

maps, 7
Margaret Lake, 75
Marian Lake, 53
McDonald Creek Drainage, 82–91
McDonald Creek, 80, 82
McGee Creek, 56
Medicine Bow Creek, 103
Medicine Grizzly Lake, 116, 118
Medicine Owl Lake, 103
Miche Wabun Lake, 74
Middle Fork of the Flathead River,
  128–29, 132–134, 136
Middle Fork of the Flathead River
  Drainage, 128–44
Middle Quartz Lake, 49
Midvale Creek, 125
Mineral Creek, 90–91
Missouri River, 13
Moccasin Creek River Access, 134
Mokawanis Lake, 76
Mokawanis River, 75
Morning Star Lake, 116
mountain whitefish, 26–27
Muir Creek, 139

N

Nahsukin Lake, 68
Natahki Lake, 110
National Park Service, 3, 16
No Name Lake, 124–25
North Fork of Cut Bank Creek, 114
North Fork of Cut Bank Creek
  Drainage, 114–18
North Fork of the Belly River, 74
North Fork of the Flathead River,
  32–39

North Fork of the Flathead River
  Drainage, 32–59
northern pike, 27–28
Numa Creek, 44
Numa Lake, 44
Nyack Creek, 141
Nyack Lakes, 140

O

Oldman Lake, 17, 122, 124
Ole Creek, 136–37
Ole Lake, 1, 17, 137–38
Olson Creek, 64
Otatso Creek, 112
Otatso Lakes, 112
Otokomi Lake, 100–101

P

Paola Creek River Access, 132–33
Paradise Creek, 125
Park Creek, 139
Parke Creek, 43
Pass Creek, 67–68
permits, 7–8
Pinchot Creek, 140
Pitamakan Lake, 114
Pocket Creek, 46
Pocket Lake, 46
Poia Lake, 111
Polebridge River Access, 36–37
Pray Lake, 121
presentation
  in lakes, 18
in rivers, 14–15
Ptarmigan Lake, 109

Q

Quartz Creek, 48
Quartz Lake, 49–50

R

Railroad Creek, 126
rainbow trout, 2, 15, 28
Red Eagle Lake, 102–3
Red Eagle Creek, 101–2

Red Medicine Bow Creek, 43
Red Rock Lake, 108
Redhorn Lake, 68
regulations, 7–9
Reynolds Creek, 98
rivers, 13–15
  number of, 16
  access to, 16–17
  strategies for, 17–18
  presentation, 18
Rogers Lake, 56
Rose Creek, 101
Rubideau Creek, 144
Ruger Lake, 55
Running Crane Lakes, 118

S

Sage Creek, 40
Saint Mary Lake, 18, 93, 97–98
Saint Mary River, 13, 92
Saint Mary River Drainage, 92–113
Saint Mary Visitor Center, 9
Shaheeya Lake, 65
Site Description, 5
Siyeh Creek, 98
Sky Lake, 124
Slide Lake, 112
Snow Moon Lake, 105
Snyder Creek, 87
South Fork of Valentine Creek, 68
spin-fishing, 15, 18
Sprague Creek, 85
Spruce Creek, 40
Starvation Creek, 41
Stimson Lake, 140
Stoney Indian Lake, 67
Street Creek, 65
Striped Elk Lake, 139
Stump Lake, 106
Sue Lake, 74
Summit Creek, 127
Summit Lake, 126
Swiftcurrent Creek, 107
Swiftcurrent Lake, 109–10
Swiftcurrent Ridge Lake, 111

T

Thomson Creek, 141
Three Bears Lake, 126-27
topographic maps, 4, 7
treble hooks, 14
Trout Lake, 56–57
Twin Lakes, 98
Two Medicine Lake, 119, 121
Two Medicine River Drainage,
   119–27
Two Medicine River, 119

U

U.S. Geologic Survey USGS, 7
Universal Transverse Mercator
   UTM, 4
Unnamed Lakes
   Above Ipasha Lake, 93
   Above Marian Lake, 54
   Adair Pond, 54
   Allen Mountain Ponds, 105
   Amphitheater Basin, 114
   Anaconda Pond, 54
   Below Brave Dog Mountain, 138
   Below Cloudcroft Peak, 140
   Below Flattop Ridge, 104
   Below Mount Wilbur, 109
   Below Red Mountain, 124
   Below Rising Wolf #1, 124
   Below Rising Wolf #2, 124
   Below Sperry Glacier, 89
   Below Sun Glacier, 78
   Below Trapper Peak, 54
   Below Wynn Mountain, 104
   Boulder Ridge #1, 104
   Boulder Ridge #2, 104
   Lower Bowman, 47
   Lower Nahsukin, 68
   Salvage Basin, 139
   Sherburne South Shore Pond, 111
   South Fork of Railroad Creek, 126
   Sperry Campground Pond, 89
   Stimson Creek, 141
   Thunderbird Pond
   Upper Divide Creek Lakes, 103
   Upper Nahsukin, 68

   Upper Ole Creek, 136
   Upper Two Medicine Pond, 122
   Yellow Mountain Pond, 112
   Below Medicine Grizzly Peak, 118
   Thomson Lakes #1 and #2
Unnamed Ponds
   Glacier Rim Area, 59
   Lime Springs, 59
Upper Bullhead Lake, 107
Upper Grinnell Lake, 106
Upper Howe Lake, 84–85
Upper Kintla Lake, 42
Upper Lake Isabel, 138
Upper Snyder Lake, 88
Upper Two Medicine Lake, 121–22

V

vacation planning, 11–12
Valentine Creek, 69
Virginia Creek, 98

W

Wahseeja Lake, 65
Walton Creek, 143
Waterton Lakes, 18, 60, 62–63
Waterton River, 13, 60
Waterton River Drainage, 60–69
waypoints, 4
West Glacier River Access, 134, 136
western cutthroat trout, 2, 29
Whitecrow Creek, 74
whitefish, 15
   lake, 26
   mountain, 26–27
Wilbur Creek, 109
Windmaker Lake, 107
Winona Lake, 48

Y

Yellowstone cutthroat trout, 2,
   29–30
Young Man Lake, 124

About the Author

Russ Schneider was born in Helena, Montana, in 1972 and grew up fishing the mountain lakes and streams of the Beartooths, the Lamar Valley in Yellowstone, and the North Fork Lakes of Glacier National Park. He revised Falcon's *Hiking Montana* in 1993, was a contributing author to *Hiking Yellowstone* in 1996, and authored *Hiking the Columbia River Gorge,* also in 1996. He revised *The Angler's Guide to Montana,* now titled *Fishing Montana,* and he co-edited *Backpacking Tips* in 1998. He has worked as a fishing, hiking, and rafting guide for Glacier Wilderness Guides in West Glacier since 1994. He writes out of Whitefish, Montana, where he makes regular trips to the park with his wife, Kim.

Visit the premiere outdoor online community ...

FALCON GUIDES®

Search

HOME   ABOUT US   CONTACT US   BOOKS   BLOGS   PHOTOS   TRAIL FINDER

The Art of Cycling
Bicycling in Traffic
Part one: Beyond the Vehicular Cycling Principle

HIKING WITH KIDS

HAPPY TRAILS Hiking in the Great Outdoors is a simple gift we all can give our children, grandchildren, and young friends. Unlike playing music, writing poetry, painting pictures, or other activities that also can fill your soul, hiking does not require any special skill. All you need to do is put one foot in front of the other in the outdoors, repeatedly. And breathe deeply.

◯ **LEARN MORE**

FEATURED NEW BOOK

SCAVENGER HIKE ADVENTURES: GREAT SMOKY MOUNTAINS NATIONAL PARK

A Totally New Interactive Hiking Guide

Introducing a brand new genre of hiking guide. Readers follow clues to find over 200 hidden natural and historic treasures on as many as 14 easy, moderate, and extreme hikes national parks. Follow the clues and find such things as a tree clawed open by a bear searching for food, an ancient Indian footpath, the remains of an old Model T Ford deep in the forest, and over 200 other unusual treasures.

◯ **CLICK HERE TO FIND OUT MORE**

RECENT BLOG POSTS

- A Dry River
- Stat-mongering -- Look Out!
- Lizard Man
- Tropical Tip of Texas
- Lions And Snakes and Bears...Oh My! "Don's PCT Update"
- Bikin' in C'ville
- The Red Store
- Journey to Idyllwild
- A Spring Quandary
- Whew!! Rocky Mountain book is printed I'm going camping!!

more

EXPERT BLOGS

- Arrowleaf Balsamroot—Another
  By: Bert Gildart
- Splitter camps #2
  By: Katie Brown
- Splitter camp
  By: Katie Brown
- Alaska Boating Adventure

outfit your mind

- Chris Sharma
- Beth Rodden
- Dean Potter
- Jason Kehl
- Josh Wharton
- Steph Davis

falcon.com